Milan

Text by Susie Boulton
Edited by Anna Tyler
Principal Photographer: Glyn Genin
Series Editor: Tony Halliday

Berlitz® POCKET GUIDE
Milan

First Edition 2007

NO part of this book may be reproduced, stored in a retrieval system or transmitted in any form or means electronic, mechanical, photocopying, recording or otherwise, without prior written permission from Berlitz Publishing. Brief text quotations with use of photographs are exempted for book review purposes only.

PHOTOGRAPHY
All photography by Glyn Genin except: 13, 14, 16, 29, 36, 46, 51, 61, 72, 75, 79, 80, 81 Jerry Dennis; 21 Sergio Piumatti; 55 Jurgen Becker/Museo Poldi Pezzoli; 59 Bridgeman Art Library; 62, 103 Ros Miller; 90 Matteo Bazzi/AFP/Getty Images.
Cover: Cogoli Franco/4 Corners Images

CONTACTING THE EDITORS
Every effort has been made to provide accurate information in this publication, but changes are inevitable. The publisher cannot be responsible for any resulting loss, inconvenience or injury. We would appreciate it if readers would call our attention to any errors or outdated information by contacting Berlitz Publishing, PO Box 7910, London SE1 1WE, England.
Fax: (44) 20 7403 0290
Email: berlitz@apaguide.co.uk
<www.berlitzpublishing.com>

All Rights Reserved

© *2007 Apa Publications GmbH & Co.*
Verlag KG, Singapore Branch, Singapore

Printed in Singapore by Insight Print Services (Pte) Ltd, 38 Joo Koon Road, Singapore 628990.
Tel: (65) 6865-1600. Fax: (65) 6861-6438

Berlitz Trademark Reg. U.S. Patent Office and other countries. Marca Registrada

La Galleria's chic boutiques and cafés have elegant belle-époque facades (page 33)

The Pinacoteca di Brera (page 48) houses one of the finest collections of Italian works of art, including *The Kiss*

Basilica di Sant' Ambrogio (page 65) is Milan's loveliest church

TOP TEN ATTRACTIONS

La Scala (page 34), Milan's world-famous opera house, has been restored to its full opulence

Markets, restaurants and cafés line the busy bohemian Navigli quarter of old canals (page 66)

Walk among the spires and statues on the rooftop of the Duomo (page 25), the third-largest cathedral in Europe, towering over the centre of Milan

Leonardo da Vinci's *The Last Supper* (page 58) is the jewel in the crown of Milan's many attractions

The priceless collection of art at the Museo Poldi Pezzoli (page 54) includes this delightful portrait

Castello Sforzesco (page 40) now has several museums

All the big names in fashion have shops in the Quadrilatero d'Oro (page 52)

CONTENTS

Introduction 7

A Brief History 13

Where to Go 25

A ➤ in the text denotes a highly recommended sight

Duomo and Historic Centre 25
Duomo 25, The Duomo Interior 28, Piazza del Duomo 30, Galleria Vittorio Emanuele II 33, Teatro alla Scala 34, Piazza Mercanti 36, Pinacoteca Ambrosiana 38, Santa Maria Presso San Satiro 39

Castello Sforzesco and the Northwest 40
Castello Sforzesco 40, Castle Museums 42, Parco Sempione 45, Cimitero Monumentale 47

The Brera 48
Pinacoteca di Brera 48, Churches of the Brera 51

Northeast of the Duomo 52
Quadrilatero d'Oro 52, Museo Bagatti Valsecchi 53, Museo Poldi Pezzoli 54, History Museums 55, Giardini Pubblici 56

West of Centre 58
The Last Supper 58, Santa Maria delle Grazie 61, Science Museum 62, Museo Archeologico and San Maurizio 63, Basilica di Sant'Ambrogio 65

South Milan: Porta Ticinese and Navigli ... 66
The Navigli 66, The Navigli Today 68, Ancient Basilicas 70, Around the University 74

Excursions from Milan 76
Chiaravalle Abbey 76, Pavia 77, Certosa di Pavia 78, Monza 80

What to Do 83

Shopping 83

Entertainment 88

Sport 93

Children 94

Eating Out 96

Handy Travel Tips 106

Hotels and Restaurants 128

Index 143

Fact Sheets
The Rise of Milan's Fashion Houses 8
Sant'Ambrogio 15
Historical Landmarks 23
Restoring La Scala 34
An Enduring Logo 40
Grand Hotel et de Milan 54
Visiting *The Last Supper* 60
The Horse That Never Was 63
Shopping Knowledge 86
Calendar of Events 95
Milanese Brunch 102

MILAN AND THE MILANESE

The old saying goes that for every church in Rome there's a bank in Milan. As the financial and economic powerhouse of Italy, the northern city prides itself on efficiency and energy, and regards the Romans as idle and unproductive, distracted by the southern sun and gagged by the Vatican. Understandably perhaps, Milan sees itself as the true capital of Italy. Not only is it the industrial and financial capital, but it has forged ahead to become the country's most dynamic and influential city.

Since the 1980s, it has been the leading centre of fashion, drawing huge numbers of visitors – many celebrities among them – to the fashion fairs and the flagship stores of Armani, Prada and other top designers. It is also the capital of publishing, media and design. Even on the football scene it eclipses the rest of Italy, boasting two of the world's top teams. But to the Romans it's a city with a misty grey climate, populated by workaholics who are dedicated purely to financial gain.

Work Hard and Play Hard

Milan certainly has a hard-work ethic, and is more in tune with a Northern European business centre than the typical Italian city of sunny piazzas and stunning monuments. But it is by no means a city of all work and no play. The lunch hours may be brief (there is nowadays a proliferation of daytime fast-food outlets) and *la dolce vita* is not played out in the same way as it is down south. But the after-work Happy Hour *aperitivo* has become very much a Milanese way of life. Stylish bars and cafés serve a sensational range of cocktails, with *stuzzichini* (snacks) and elegant canapés. Many of these

Up among the pinnacles of the Duomo roof

venues become clubs or discos after 11pm, opening until the early hours of the morning. Offering the most vibrant nightlife in Italy, Milan attracts clubbers from all corners of the country. Not surprisingly, the city also offers a wealth of culinary treats, from delicious creamy risottos and Lombard pasta specialities, *prosciutto crudo*, mountain hams, abundant fish and local wines and cheeses, to a large variety of ethnic fare.

La Bella Figura

The city is synonymous with fashion, and the Milanese enjoy spending large amounts of their hard-earned cash on cutting-edge fashions. Twice a year, at the opening of the world-famous fashion fairs, the Italian and international paparazzi

The Rise of Milan's Fashion Houses

Milan has a long tradition of fashion and clothing, producing fine fabrics since the 13th century, but it was not until the the latter half of the last century that the city became a world centre for fashion design. Florence had previously taken centre stage, but many of its haute couturiers, constrained by the elitist traditions and rigid rules of the Pitti Palace shows, transferred to Milan. From the 1970s, shows took place at the Fiera, and the following two decades saw Milan's meteoric rise to Europe's capital of fashion.

By the end of the decade, four of its designers – Armani, Versace, Prada and Dolce & Gabbana – were ranked in the world's top 10 fashion houses. Milan's image transformed from a dull industrial metropolis to an exclusive shopping Mecca. Prêt-à-porter collections revolutionised the industry, filling the gap for chic but accessible leisurewear for the affluent. Giorgio Armani, who started his company in 1975, was one of the first to introduce a prêt-à-porter collection. In 2002 he commissioned the Japanese architect Tadao Ando to convert a former chocolate factory in Milan to the Armani headquarters, complete with theatre.

descend on the city to shoot next season's collections; hip hotels with cool cocktail bars are reserved a year in advance, stylish restaurants and sushi bars are packed out with celebrities, supermodels and fashion aficionados, while parties take place throughout the city.

But at any time of year the locals cut a *bella figura,* and the stunningly chic Quadrilatero d'Oro (Golden Rectangle), where the designer shops are concentrated, provides a non-stop fashion show.

A style-conscious local

While you don't need to be kitted out in the latest Gucci shades or Armani suit, it helps to leave your tracksuits and trainers at home or keep them for the jogging paths in the Giardini Pubblici.

The stores are more like art galleries than shops, and range from little boutiques in *palazzi* to megastores where you can do far more than shop for fashions. At the glamorous Dolce & Gabbana on Corso Venezia, men's fashions come with a barber, beauty farm and Martini bar. Armani combines clothes and accessories with furnishings, a Sony store, books, chocolates, flowers and an Armani café and Nobu restaurant. Prices at these ultra-elegant stores are not for the faint-hearted, but if your credit card won't stretch to cutting-edge collections, there are plenty of more affordable fashions in the city centre, as well as the arty boutiques of the Brera or Ticinese quarters.

Milan is the number-one city in Italy for design as well as fashion. Every April, 200,000 international visitors flock to the trade fair for the fashionable Salone Internazionale del Mobile, the furniture and design exhibition. Milan's Triennale in Parco Sempione, home to the International Design Show, hosts spectacular design and architecture exhibitions and is soon to become a design museum. The major international fashion, furniture and design shows now take place at Massimiliano Fuksas's bold new trade fair complex outside the centre in Rho-Pero. Constructed in just two years on the site of a former oil refinery, the Fiera Milano covers 2 million square metres, and focuses on a stunning sail-shaped roof of steel and glass.

Cultural Legacy

Milan may not offer the rich architectural heritage or homogeneity of, say, Florence or Venice, but it has a number of fine churches and galleries, a historic castle and one of the world's most prestigious opera houses. At its centre rises one of Europe's largest and most sumptuous Gothic churches, and in the Refectory of Santa Maria delle Grazie hangs what is arguably the most revered image in the Western world: Leonardo da Vinci's *The Last Supper*. Art museums range from the major collection of Italian paintings in the Pinacoteca di Brera to modern galleries at the cutting edge of contemporary art.

Though little survives of medieval Milan, you can see what it was once like in the 13th-century Piazza Mercanti, which holds the fine Palazzo della Ragione, dating from 1233. During the Renaissance, Milan became a centre of art and culture, where geniuses such as Leonardo and Bramante were commissioned to restore and create monuments, and adorn palaces and churches with great works of art. Key navigable waterways were created to link to the River Ticino in Switzerland and enable huge blocks of marble to be carried for the Duomo.

> **The Milanese refer to themselves as Ambrosiani, after Sant' Ambrogio (St Ambrose), patron saint of the city.**

A good tram system flows in and out of the old walled city

Most of the city centre comprises imposing boulevards and stately *palazzi* created under three and a half centuries of foreign rule. The most conspicuous legacy dates from the Austrian occupation, which saw the construction of neo-classical monuments such as the Teatro alla Scala, the Palazzo Reale (Royal Palace) and Brera Academy of Fine Arts.

Until the 1950s, the tallest building in the city's skyline was the Duomo. Now several modern skyscrapers supersede it. At 127m (417ft), the slim and graceful Pirelli Tower, close to the central station, is the highest structure. Designed by Milanese architect Gio Ponti, with Pier Luigi Nervi, and built in 1960 on the site of the first Pirelli tyre factory, it became a symbol of the nation's economic revival, and is now the headquarters of the Lombardy regional government.

The markets, antiques and artisan-based shops of Milan's arty Brera neighbourhood and bohemian Navigli quarter showcase the creative side of this modern business city.

Population and Layout

Lying 50km (30 miles) south of the Alps in the heavily developed Po Valley, Milan is the capital of Lombardy, the most populated and developed region in Italy. The city covers an area of around 180 sq km (70 sq miles) and has a population of around 1.3 million, making it the second-largest city in Italy. With the suburbs included, the number swells to over 4.25 million.

A smart arcade in central Milan

The city is contained within a series of concentric circles radiating from the centre. The main historical monuments, museums, galleries and exclusive shops are conveniently concentrated within the inner ring of boulevards, formerly a circle of canals (the Cerchia dei Navigli). The Spanish constructed a second perimeter in the mid-16th-century by building city walls, extending 11km (7 miles) around the city and incorporating four main gateways. By the end of the 19th century, the city was bursting at the seams again, and the Spanish bastions and the gateways were gradually demolished to push the city further out. Today, the outermost ring road, the Circonvallazione Esterna, encompasses residential suburbs and industrial estates. The city is still expanding, particularly northwards.

Milan's location makes it an ideal destination for excursions. It has good rail and road links with the historic cities of Lombardy such as Pavia, Bergamo and Brescia; and should you need a break from bustling streets and cultural overload you can quickly escape – like the Milanese – to the tranquillity of the lakes and mountains, less than an hour away.

A BRIEF HISTORY

Milan has a far longer history than its modern appearance might lead you to believe. Strategically located on the trade route from the Alps to Rome, the city inevitably suffered the rampages of a succession of foreign rulers. The Celts were the first to invade, in the 6th century BC, followed by Romans, Huns, Goths, Lombards, Spaniards, Austrians and French. Despite invasions, sieges, plagues and, most recently, the bombardments of World War II, Milan has managed to emerge as Italy's wealthiest and most dynamic city.

Ancient Mediolanum

The origin of the city's ancient name, 'Mediolanum', remains something of a mystery. It could simply have derived from the Celtic name for the settlement, Medelhan, meaning 'in the middle of the plain', or, more picturesquely, from the rough Latin translation of Mediolanum, 'wool in the middle', which refers back to the legend of the half-woolly wild boar that the Celts discovered in Milan in ancient times. According to Latin historian Titus Livius (Livy), the foundation stone of Milan was laid in 603BC by a Celtic tribe from Gaul.

Emperor Constantine

Sant'Ambrogio, bishop of Milan

The Romans called this wild barbaric region Gallia Cisalpina – Gaul this side of the Alps. In 222BC they put an end to Celtic forays, conquering Milan and other settlements of the Po Valley. Under Roman rule Milan became a thriving commercial centre, and in AD286, when Emperor Diocletian divided the Roman Empire, the town became the administrative seat of the West.

In 313 Constantine the Great, ruler of the Western Roman Empire, signed the crucial Edict of Milan, granting Christians religious freedom. Milan became a leading religious centre, consolidating Christianity and fostering new forms of religious architecture. This was largely thanks to the influence of its first bishop, Ambrogio.

Huns, Goths and Lombards

The following centuries saw a decline in the city's fortunes as it was ravaged by waves of invaders. First came Attila the Hun, destroying Milan in 452. Following the breakdown of the Roman Empire in the West a quarter of a century later, Milan, along with the rest of Italy, was subject to invasions by the Goths. Odoacer, a general in the army of the Western Roman Empire, crowned himself king in 476 at Italy's new capital at Pavia but was murdered at a banquet by his rival, Theodoric the Ostrogoth, who went on to have a successful 40-year reign. Italy was invaded by the Eastern Empire in 536, and Milan was rescued from the barbarians by General

Belisarius during the Imperial Restoration. But in 563 the city finally fell to the Goths and was razed to the ground.

Just five years later, another warfaring Germanic tribe, the brutal Longobardi (Lombards), descended on the region and seized the main cities north of the Po. Their leader, King Alboin, established his court at Pavia but was murdered by his wife, Rosamunda (whom he had forced to drink wine from her dead father's skull). However, the Lombards gradually renounced their barbarian ways and were absorbed into the local population, adopting Roman life and customs, freely intermarrying and in many cases converting to Christianity.

Lombardy was formally integrated into Christendom when it became part of the Carolingian Empire under Charlemagne. The city then enjoyed a sustained period of vitality, particularly in the late 9th and 10th centuries when trade prospered and splendid churches were constructed.

Sant'Ambrogio

Legend has it that shortly after Ambrogio's birth in 340 a swarm of bees descended on the infant's face, leaving a drop of honey on his lips and prophesying his future gift as a (honey-tongued) orator (hence the bees and beehives in the saint's iconography). Ambrogio was born in Trier, Germany, and raised in Rome. His career saw a dramatic leap in 374, from a local administrator of Liguria and Emilia to the first Bishop of Milan, despite a lack of theological training.

During his 20 years as bishop, Ambrogio zealously campaigned against Arianism and heresy. Among his many converts to Christianity was St Augustine, whom he baptised in 387. Four great basilicas, including Sant'Ambrogio, were founded in Milan during his time as bishop. He was made patron saint of the city, and is celebrated every 7 December with the grand opening of the La Scala opera season and a popular two-day market around the Basilica di Sant'Ambrogio.

Tower at Castello Sforzesco

The Commune of Milan

Milan was now free to become a commune – or free city state. Struggle ensued for supremacy between the city and other leading centres of Lombardy. Milan prevailed in wars with Pavia, Cremona, Como and Lodi, but the destruction of Como gave the Holy Roman Emperor, Frederick Barbarossa, the pretext again to bring back the city under imperial power. A nine-month siege followed, the city fell in 1162, and many of the inhabitants were forced to flee to the countryside.

Five years later Milan joined with other communes in the new Lombard League, the northern Italian separatist movement which defeated Barbarossa at Legnano, northwest of Milan, in 1176. Barbarossa was forced to sign the Peace of Constance in 1183, which formally established the authority and independence of the communes of northern Italy, including Milan.

The Visconti and Sforza

Internal power struggles led to the decline of the communes, and the 13th century saw the rise to power of the great family dynasties. In 1262 the Pope appointed Ottone Visconti as archbishop to counterbalance the power of the Torriani family who were ruling Milan. The Visconti, largely comprising the aristocracy, took the name of Ghibellines (pro the German emperor), the Torriani, leaders of the popular forces, the Guelphs (pro the Pope). Ottone won a great battle against his rival dynasty at Desio in 1277 and claimed the ancient temporal powers of the archbishops of Milan.

From 1395, the Visconti were dukes of the city, and it was under Gian Galeazzo Visconti (1351–1402) that the duchy reached its zenith. By military conquest and diplomacy, he expanded Milan's territories to cover most of northern Italy, extending as far as Pisa, Siena, Perugia and Bologna. However, as the duke was beginning to muster his forces against Florence, he was struck down by the plague and died. A man of great cultural and religious ambition, Gian Galeazzo saw the foundation of Milan's cathedral and castle and the great Certosa (Carthusian monastery) at Pavia.

In 1447, following a threat from a Venetian army, his son, Filippo Maria, sought military assistance from his son-in-law, the *condottiere* (mercenary) Francesco Sforza. This heralded a century of rule by the next great family dynasty, the Sforzas. Francesco's eldest son, Galeazzo Maria Sforza, though extravagant and dissolute, was an able leader who introduced the cultivation of rice and mulberries. Under his rule, industry also flourished, particularly the manufacture of textiles and arms.

The Visconti coat of arms

Furthermore, he initiated the patronage of leading artists and scholars, for which the Sforzas were to become renowned. The duke was murdered in 1476 on the steps of Milan's San Gottardo in Corte chapel by a small group of aggrieved court officials.

Ludovico il Moro

The most celebrated of the Sforza rulers was Ludovico, who usurped power through the regency of his seven-year-old nephew, Gian Galeazzo Maria. Known as Ludovico il Moro (the Moor) on account of his swarthy complexion and black hair, he was one of the great princes of the Renaissance. In his day, there were five great superpowers in Italian politics: the Papacy, the kingdom of Naples and Sicily, Florence, Venice and Milan. It was the era of equilibrium politics, when each superstate strived for survival or supremacy by subtle and sometimes duplicitous diplomacy. Ludovico survived by his mastery of it. He hated the burgeoning power of his nearest rival, Venice, but courted the support of Florence. He struck alliances with the two great powers of Continental Europe, France and the Holy Roman Empire, to prevent reinstatement of the true heir to the dukedom. Later he made an alliance with Venice against France with the marriage of his niece, Bianca Maria, to the Holy Roman Emperor, Maximilian, and chose for himself the beautiful 15-year-old Beatrice d'Este, daughter of the Duke of Ferrara. From Maximilian he purchased the dukedom of Milan and, with his wife, maintained one of the most elegant courts in Europe.

Leonardo da Vinci

Under Ludovico's patronage leading artists and architects were commissioned to restore and create monuments and adorn palaces and churches. The Tuscan-born, multi-talented Leonardo da Vinci ran a flourishing studio of pupils, worked as technical adviser and military architect to the duke, designed court festivals and produced most of his groundbreaking artistic, scientific and medical studies. *The Last Supper* is one of the few of his paintings that survive in the city.

Initiating the chaotic period of European intervention in Italian politics, Charles VIII of France attempted to conquer Naples in 1494, prompting Ludovico to join a Venetian alliance to expel the French from Italy. On Charles's death, Louis XII claimed the duchy of Milan as a descendant of the first Visconti duke. Ludovico was expelled, with the encouragement of the populace who by now had tired of his policy of high taxation. In 1500 he attempted to reclaim the city, but his conscript Swiss and German armies refused to support him when the critical moment came, and he was exiled to France, where he spent the rest of his life.

Foreign Intervention

The great struggle between France and Habsburg Spain for dominance in Italy effectively ended at the battle of Pavia in 1525, when the French were expelled from the duchy of Milan. The state of Milan was briefly restored to the Sforza dynasty, but, on the death of Francesco II in 1535, the duchy fell under the domination of the Spanish Habsburg emperor Charles V, who later granted it to his son, the future Philip II of Spain. From the golden age of the duchy, Milan underwent the dark age of Spanish domination. It was to last 170 years – an era of political, commercial and cultural stagnation, reaching its lowest ebb with the devastating plague of 1630.

Economic revival had to wait until the Spanish rulers were driven out by the Austrians in the War of the Spanish Succes-

> The classic novel, *I Promessi Sposi (The Betrothed)*, by the Milanese author Alessandro Manzoni, is a vivid portrayal of Milan under Spanish rule. It is set in 1628–31, when 60,000 citizens were struck down by the devastating 'Manzonian' plague.

sion. Their occupation was to last, almost uninterrupted, from 1706 until 1859. Although notoriously despotic, the rulers collaborated with the emerging commercial classes, fostering 50 years of enlightenment and growth. The reign of the enlightened Empress Maria Theresa saw major economic and social reforms, the rise of splendid neoclassical buildings and palaces such as the Teatro alla Scala, and the rebuilding of the Palazzo Reale (Royal Palace).

The French returned in 1796, with Napoleon Bonaparte's armies sweeping into Milan. Napoleon had the full support of the Milanese bourgeoisie, and the Austrians were chased out. Milan became capital of the Cisalpine Republic, and Napoleon was crowned king of Italy in the Duomo in 1805. But Milan – along with the rest of Lombardy and most of Italy – was soon to fall again to the Austrians. This time it was a generally hated regime, and in 1848, when revolution was sweeping through Italy, Milan was the scene of the Cinque Giornate (Five Days) revolt. Control was soon regained, but by then the tide of the Risorgimento (Italian Unification Movement) was virtually unstoppable. In 1859 the troops of Vittorio Emanuele and Napoleon III of France defeated the Austrians at Magenta and Solferino, and entered Milan in triumph.

Unification to Present Day

By 1870 Italy was finally united. Vittorio Emanuele became the first king of Italy, and Rome was declared capital of the new kingdom. Rapid growth and industrialisation characterised the post-unification period. Milan became the economic and cultural capital of Italy, and over a period of 50 years the population trebled in size. But with growth came social tension, and the first socialist party, the Partito Operaio Italiano, was founded in Milan in 1882. Following World War I, political and economic problems led to the birth of the new and powerful force of Fascism. It was in Milan that Mussolini created the Fasci di Combattimento in 1919, the nucleus of Europe's first Fascist party. Milan was part of Mussolini's unsuccessful puppet government at Salò on Lake Garda from 1943–5. Following his capture and execution in 1945, he was brought to Milan and put on display, alongside his mistress, Clara Petacci, at a petrol station in Piazzale Loreto.

As a key industrial centre, Milan was the target of devastating bombardments from Allied air raids during World War II. Large numbers of significant buildings were damaged beyond repair. A major reconstruction programme followed,

Piazza della Scala as it was in 1880

and in the 1950s the city became an industrial powerhouse, forming with Genoa and Turin the 'Industrial Triangle' of Italy. Migrants flocked in from southern Italy, taking up jobs in the factories of Fiat, Alfa Romeo and Pirelli. During the 1960s the emphasis on industry moved to service industries. By the 1980s Milan was not only Italy's leading centre for commerce and finance but the country's capital for publishing, media, fashion and design.

But alongside the economic boom came political scandal, organised crime and terrorism. On 12 December 1969 a bomb exploded in Milan's Piazza Fontana, killing 16 and heralding a decade of terrorist activity, from both the left and the right. In the early 1990s the city was the focus of the great political scandal dubbed *Tangentopoli* (Bribesville). Extensive investigations, which became known as the *Mani Pulite* (Clean Hands), exposed political corruption on a massive scale, and led to the accusation of eight former prime ministers and around 5,000 businessmen.

In 2006 Silvio Berlusconi, the self-made Milanese media tycoon, was ousted from power by the centre-left alliance headed by Romano Prodi. Notorious for his shady dealings, Berlusconi is still facing charges of fraud and money-laundering. Prodi has inherited from him a sluggish economy, high unemployment and a mountain of public debt.

On the streets of stylish Milan, however, where designer-clad locals work hard and play hard, there are no visible signs that the city is feeling the pinch.

A Milanese cyclist

Historical Landmarks

603BC Milan founded by the Gauls.
222BC Romans occupy Milan.
AD286 Milan becomes capital of the Western Roman Empire.
452 Attila the Hun plunders Milan.
563 Milan is razed by the Goths.
568 Invasion of Lombards.
774 Charlemagne brings Lombard rule to an end.
1045 Milan constitutes itself a free commune.
1162 Frederick Barbarossa brings the city under imperial control.
1176 Lombard League defeats Barbarossa at Legnano.
1183 Milan (and other northern Italian cities) regains independence.
1262 Rise of the Visconti dynasty.
1447 Rise of the Sforza dynasty; Milan becomes one of the leading cities of the Renaissance.
1535 Milan falls to Spain.
1629–31 Milan is devastated by the plague.
1706 Milan is ceded to Austria.
1796 Napoleon makes Milan capital of his Cisalpine Republic.
1815 Congress of Vienna gives Milan again to the Austrians.
1848 Cinque Giornate revolt in Milan; Austrians re-enter Milan.
1859 Austrians defeated at the battle of Magenta – troops of Vittorio Emanuele and France re-enter Milan.
1919 Mussolini founds the first Fascist party in Milan.
1943 Milan suffers heavy bombardment in World War II.
1945 Mussolini is executed and his body strung up in Milan.
2001 Coalition headed by Milan's Silvio Berlusconi wins general election.
2002 The euro becomes the official Italian currency.
2004 The Teatro alla Scala reopens after a three-year renovation.
2006 Berlusconi's Forza Italia party is narrowly defeated by Romano Prodi's centre-left alliance.
2007 Prodi resigns as prime minister after nine months (making 60 Italian governments since 1945), but is reinstated three days later.

WHERE TO GO

The historic heart of the city is surprisingly compact, and most of the sights can be covered on foot. The main arteries fan out from the great Gothic Duomo and La Scala opera house: northwest to the imposing Castello Sforzesco and Parco Sempione, northeast to the Quadrilatero d'Oro fashion district, north to the arty neighbourhood of the Brera. To the west lies the smart Corso Magenta, with Santa Maria delle Grazie's *The Last Supper* by Leonardo, and to the south, the hip Navigli canal quarter. The main attractions of the city can be covered in a couple of days, either on foot or with short journeys on trams, buses or by metro. For locations further afield the fastest access is via the metro.

The Duomo, the geographical and spiritual heart of the city, is a natural magnet and the best place to start exploring.

DUOMO AND HISTORIC CENTRE

Duomo

Dominating the heart of the city, and soaring over the central square, is the Gothic **Duomo** (cathedral: open daily 7am–7pm; treasury and crypt: 9am–5.15pm, 4.15pm winter; baptistery: 10am–noon, 3–7pm; roof: 9am–5.45pm, 4.15pm winter; admission fee for treasury, baptistery and roof; cathedral free of charge; <www.duomomilano.it>).

Nothing quite prepares you for the first sight of the monumental facade. This is the third-largest church in Europe, after the cathedral of Seville and St Peter's in Rome. The area covers 12,000 sq m (130,000 sq ft), the capacity is around 40,000, and the facade is adorned with a forest of

The entrance to the lofty Galleria from Piazza del Duomo

3,000 statues, 135 spires and 96 gargoyles. (At present it is also adorned with scaffolding, and will be until 2008.)

Begun in 1386, the Duomo was the brainchild of Duke Gian Galeazzo Visconti, whose aim was to create the greatest church in Christendom. The then bishop of Milan, Antonio da Saluzzo, declared a Jubilee to persuade the Milanese to help fund or assist the colossal project. Armourers, drapers, bootmakers and other artisans all lent their voluntary efforts, while French and German architects, engineers and sculptors, well versed in the Gothic tradition, were brought in to work alongside the locals. At one stage, there were around 300 sculptors from all over Europe chiselling away in the cathedral workshops.

> A much-loved symbol of the city, the Madonnina, atop the Duomo, is in fact 4.46m (14½ft) high. She was placed on the church's highest spire in 1774, and remained the highest point in the city until the Pirelli skyscraper was built in the late 1950s *(see page 11)*. The clergy were none too pleased she had lost her superior position, so a replica was placed on top of the Pirelli Tower.

The original plan was a building in Lombard terracotta, but Gian Galeazzo changed his mind and decided the entire structure was to be clad in white Candoglia marble. This entailed the construction of roads and canals to drag the great blocks of marble from the quarries near Lake Maggiore.

Despite the huge workforce it was to be more than five centuries before the

Exploring the roof terraces of the Duomo

cathedral was completed. The result is a hybrid of Renaissance, Gothic and baroque styles, with 19th-century additions. The work on the facade, which was not begun until the 17th century, gave rise to decades of controversy, and was only finished in 1812 under Napoleon.

Even on a dull day the marble facade looks strikingly white, and almost blindingly so since its 21st-century facelift. Before entering the church, take a look at the very different style of the apse. Built in 1386–1447, and decorated with sculptures and tracery, this is the oldest part of the Duomo, and one that is genuinely Gothic.

While you are at this back end of the Duomo, you should make a point of going up to the **Terrazzi** (roof terraces). You can either reach them by a lift or take the slightly cheaper and more strenuous option of clambering up the 158 steps. Apart from sensational views of the city and, on those rare, very clear days, as far as the Matterhorn, you can admire the forest of spires, statues, turrets and gargoyles, and get a closer look at the gilded figure of the **Madonnina** (Little Madonna) which crowns the cathedral.

The Duomo Interior

From the dazzling white piazza you are plunged into the dimly lit, spartan interior. The five aisles are divided by 52 colossal piers – one for every week of the year – their capitals decorated with 15th-century figures of saints and prophets. Works of art within the church include sarcophagi, funerary shrines and statues, the most famous of which is the gruesome, anatomical *Statue of St Bartholomew Flayed* (1562) in the right transept, depicting the saint carrying his own skin. At the end of the transept lies the elaborate marble tomb of Gian Giacomo Medici, by Leone Leoni (1509–90), a pupil of Michelangelo. This was commissioned in 1564 by

Inside the Duomo, where there is a pillar for every week of the year

Pope Pius IV, who was the brother of Gian Giacomo. Unconnected with the Florentine Medici and nicknamed *Il Medeghino* (Little Medico), Gian Giacomo was from a Milanese family but was banished from the city after committing a murder. He fled to Lake Como and acquired his wealth from privateering and working as a *condottiere* (mercenary) in the service of Charles V. A large sum donated to the Duomo, plus family connections, ensured this prominent funerary monument. In the Left Transept the seven-branched bronze **Trivulzio Candelabrum** is the work of a medieval goldsmith of French or German origin. The monsters and mythical figures represent the arts, crafts and virtues.

Stained-glass apse window

The church is illuminated by beautiful **stained-glass windows**, dating from the 15th–20th centuries. The oldest is the fifth window in the right-hand aisle, illustrating scenes from the *Life of Christ*. The beautiful Gothic windows of the apse are decorated by 19th-century scenes from both the Old and New Testaments. The permanently shining red light in the vault of the Duomo marks the place of a **nail** said to be from Christ's cross. On the second Sunday in September, the bishop of Milan is hoisted up to the vault to bring the nail down from its niche for public view.

A stairway behind the main altar leads down to the **Treasury**, housing a priceless collection of gold, silverwork and holy vestments. In the neighbouring **Crypt** (1606), a rock crystal urn contains the body of San Carlo Borromeo (1538–84), clad in full regalia. Archbishop and cardinal of Milan, he was a leading light of the Catholic Counter-Reformation and was canonised in 1610. A staircase near the Duomo entrance leads down to the remains of the 4th-century **Baptistery** on what was then pavement level. It was here that Sant'Ambrogio is said to have baptised St Augustine.

Piazza del Duomo

The gigantic central piazza, milling with people and pigeons, is grand in scale and awe-inspiring, but lacks the charm and laid-back atmosphere of the typical Italian piazza. There are no cafés actually on the square (though you can find them under the arcades framing it on two sides), and the hundreds of business-like Milanese that cross it daily invariably seem to be in a rush. A far more inviting and relaxing rendezvous is the Galleria Vittorio Emanuele II *(see page 33)*. The only landmark on the piazza, apart from the big red Ms of the metro, is Ercole Rosa's 1896 equestrian statue of Vittorio Emanuele II, first king of Italy, who triumphantly entered Milan in 1859.

The **Palazzo Reale** (Royal Palace) on the south side of the Duomo stands on the site of the original Broletto or town hall, destroyed by Frederick Barbarossa in 1162. It was rebuilt in 1171, then later transformed into the Ducal Palace for the Visconti and Sforza dynasties. On the occasion of Galeazzo Visconti's marriage to Beatrice d'Este in Modena, their entry into Milan was marked by eight days of sumptuous celebra-

Statue of Vittorio Emanuele II

Palazzo Reale, where a 14-year-old Mozart once performed

tions at the palace. In 1336 the **Church of San Gottardo in Corte** was built as the Visconti's private chapel. You can still see the charming colonnaded campanile rising to the rear of the palace, but the church itself was destroyed when the building was incorporated into the neoclassical palace. In 1412 the church steps were the scene of the murder of Giovanni Maria Visconti. As a consequence the family decided to reside in the safer environs of the fortified castle. Under the Sforzas a theatre was established at the palace, and in 1595 Mozart, who was only 14, performed here.

The current neoclassical aspect of the Palazzo Reale dates from the transformation during the late 18th century, when Empress Maria Theresa of Austria invited leading architects to compete in a plan to redesign the palace as the seat of the governor. The winner was Giuseppe Piermarini, who remodelled the building in the neoclassical style of the time, with sumptuously decorated rooms. The apartments and contents

> The colourful pavement mosaics under the glass dome of the Galleria depict the coat of arms of the Savoys and the symbols of four cities: Milan (red cross on a white background, *see opposite*), Turin (bull), Florence (lily) and Rome (she-wolf). Tradition has it that spinning your heels on the bull's well-worn testicles will bring good luck.

suffered major devastation during the bombardments of 1943, and have been undergoing intermittent restoration ever since.

Since the 1950s, the building has hosted a series of major exhibitions of contemporary art. Several rooms have been restored in styles which characterise court life here in 1781–1860 and can be seen in the **Museo della Reggia** (Royal Palace Museum; open Tues–Sun 9.30am–5.30pm; work is still in progress). The east wing of the Palazzo Reale houses the **Museo del Duomo** (Cathedral Museum; closed for restoration until 2008; admission fee). The collection provides a fascinating history of the construction of the Duomo, with former wooden models and plans, including a 19th-century design for a change of facade which never materialised. Original statues from the exterior of the Duomo are kept here for preservation, along with original stained glass and architectural features. There is also a section on how the Madonnina got to the top of the highest spire in 1774.

Until recently, the palace displayed various works from the Civico Museo di Arte Contemporaneo or CiMAC (Civic Museum of Contemporary Art), whose collection ranges from the avant-garde movements of the early 1900s to art from the early 1980s. The collection will be reborn as the Museo del Novecento (Museum of the 20th Century) in the adjacent Arengario building, until recently home to Milan's central tourist office. Part of the Palazzo Reale was demolished in the late 1930s to make way for this three-storey

Galleria Vittorio Emanuele II

Linking Piazza del Duomo and Piazza della Scala is the pedestrianised **Galleria Vittorio Emanuele II** (or 'La Galleria'), a light and airy glass-and-iron shopping arcade. This elegant rendezvous, known as *il salotto di Milano* (Milan's drawing room), is flanked by cafés, restaurants, bookshops and designer boutiques. Prada has been here since 1913, while Louis Vuitton and Gucci are more recent arrivals. The chic cafés and shops have belle-époque facades – even McDonald's has a certain elegance here.

The cruciform Galleria, built in honour of Austrian Emperor Franz Joseph, was the work of architect Giuseppe Mengoni, who plunged to his death in 1878 from the scaffolding on the site just a few months before it was completed. The café terraces here are great spots for watching the flow of elegant Milanese. Savini is the oldest restaurant, and has been welcoming stars from La Scala since 1867. Zucca in Galleria at the Piazza del Duomo end, where Verdi used to enjoy a drink after concerts, is a historic café where Campari was invented in 1867. It is also known

Pavement mosaic in La Galleria

for its fine interior Art Nouveau mosaics, and a medicinal-like rhubarb drink called *zucca* (ask for *uno zucca*, not *una zucca* which means a pumpkin!).

Teatro alla Scala

The sombre neoclassical facade of the world-famous opera house gives no hint of the fabulously opulent auditorium. More popularly known as **La Scala**, this is one of the world's most prestigious opera houses. Many top names in Italian opera have made their debuts here, among them Puccini, Verdi and Bellini. Commissioned in 1776–8 by Empress Maria Theresa of Austria, it was designed by Giuseppe Piermarini and built on the site of a former theatre which was destroyed by fire in 1776. The new theatre was named after the church of Santa Maria alla Scala, which originally

Restoring La Scala

In 2002 the opera house closed for a huge (and controversial) restoration and rebuilding programme. The auditorium was painstakingly restored with a wealth of gilded stuccowork, crimson damask and velvet and chandeliers, and state-of-the-art facilities were added, including screens on the back of seats to supply translated text and air conditioning. The reopening in 2004, after the three-year restoration project (and much political wrangling), was celebrated with Salieri's *Europa Riconsciuta* – a work which had not been performed here since the opening of the opera house 266 years earlier.

Opera fans should book seats for La Scala well in advance of performances. Despite the 2,000-seat capacity, the most popular operas sell out on the first day. The season starts with a grand opening and a star-studded audience on 7 December, the feast of Sant'Ambrogio, Milan's patron saint. For information on booking tickets visit <www.teatroallascala.org> and see *pages 89–90*.

La Scala's recently restored auditorium, with seating for 2,000

stood here. The theatre suffered serious damage during the 1943 air raids, but was the first structure in the city to be rebuilt. The reconstruction took less than a year, and the reopening was celebrated with a memorable concert conducted by Toscanini, the former conductor, who returned from America after a 17-year absence.

Provided there are no rehearsals going on, you can peep into the auditorium on a visit to the **Museo Teatrale alla Scala** (Scala Theatre Museum; open daily 9am–12.30pm, 1.30–5.30pm; admission fee). The neoclassical rooms display portraits and busts of famous opera singers and composers, stage designs, musical instruments and operatic memorabilia.

In the centre of **Piazza della Scala** the bearded figure on the pedestal is Leonardo da Vinci, while the figures below are four of his pupils. Facing the Teatro alla Scala, the splendid **Palazzo Marino** was built for a wealthy Genoese financier, Tommaso Marino, in 1558 and given a new facade in the late

Casa di Alessandro Manzoni

19th century. Today, this is the Town Hall, and you can peek through the grill into the Courtyard of Honour from Via Marina which leads into Piazza San Fedele.

In front of the baroque church of San Fedele stands a statue of Alessandro Manzoni (1785–1873), author of the widely acclaimed *I Promessi Sposi (The Betrothed)*. The most famous novel in 19th-century Italian literature, it is set in Lombardy during the oppressive Spanish rule in the 17th century, and vividly describes the plague of 1830 which devastated Milan. Born in Milan in 1814, Manzoni lived in the nearby Piazza Belgioioso, at the **Casa di Alessandro Manzoni** (Via Morone 1, overlooking Piazza Belgioioso; open Tues–Fri 9am–noon, 2–4pm; free) until his death after a fall on the steps of the San Fedele church. To reach the house, walk behind San Fedele into Via Omenoni, named after the eight telamones (figures as pillars) which you can't fail to miss on the **Casa degli Omenoni**.

Piazza Mercanti

In contrast to the Piazza del Duomo, the **Piazza Mercanti** near by is a small, intimate square which was left relatively unscathed by 19th-century ravages and 20th-century bombs. The former political and administrative centre of the city, it is only half of its original size (the square formerly stretched to what is today the Via Mercanti), but it preserves the medieval **Palazzo della Ragione** (1233), a fine porticoed brick building which was formerly the Broletto (law courts). It was built by Oldrado da Tresseno, the *podestà* (mayor) whom you can see depicted in an equestrian relief on the piazza side of the palace. Between the second and third arches you can see a relief of the half-woolly wild boar *(scrofa semilanuta)*, symbol of the city in ancient times. A third storey was added in 1773 to house the archives of notaries who used to draft their documents on small desks around the loggia.

On the other side of the square is the lovely Loggia degli Osii, the grey-and-white-striped marble building where banns were declared. The coats of arms on the building are those of families who lived nearby. The loggia of the Palazzo della Ragione used to shelter medieval market stalls; today temporary exhibitions take place here. On the piazza an old well survives, and tables spill on to the square from the charming Ristorante al Mercante *(see page 136)*.

An old well in the intimate Piazza Mercanti

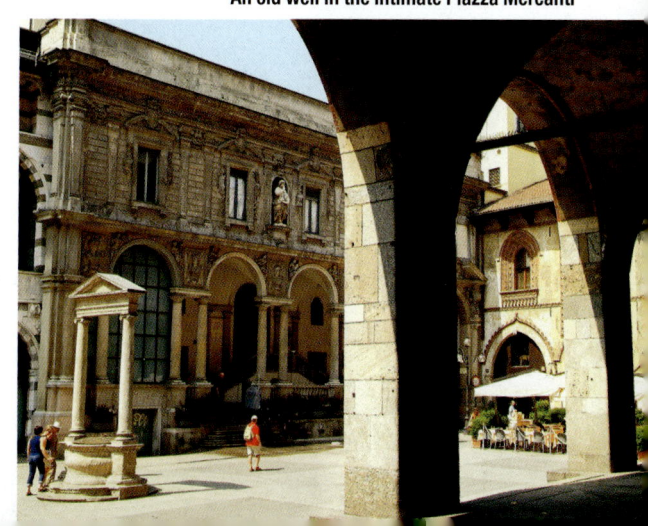

Pinacoteca Ambrosiana

In 1609 Cardinal Federico Borromeo commissioned the Biblioteca Ambrosiana (Ambrosiana Library) to house his huge collection of manuscripts, prints and books, which he had amassed from all over Europe and the Far East. This is believed to have been the first public library in Italy. Federico was also a patron of the arts, and in 1618 he donated his outstanding collection of paintings to the Ambrosiana Foundation. This was enriched by further donations over the centuries and today occupies 23 rooms of the **Pinacoteca Ambrosiana** (Ambrosiana Gallery, Piazza Pio XI; open Tues–Sun 10am–5.30pm; admission fee; <www.ambrosiana.it>). The library contains some 30,000 manuscripts and 500,000 printed volumes. Among the treasures, accessible only to scholars, is the *Codex Atlanticus*, the largest collection of Leonardo da Vinci's notes and drawings.

Ornate staircase in the Pinacoteca Ambrosiana

The highlights of the gallery are the first rooms, containing many of the works from Federico's original private collection. Masterpieces include Titian's *Adoration of the Magi* (Room 1), *The Musician* (Room 2), depicting a musician in the Sforza Court and attributed to Leonardo da Vinci, Raphael's cartoon for the *School of Athens* fresco in the Vatican (Room 5) and Caravaggio's famous *Basket of Fruit* (Room 6), of which Federico wrote, 'I would have liked to have put another similar basket next to it, but as nobody could equal the beauty and incomparable excellence of this one, it remained alone.' There are also paintings by Botticelli, Ghirlandaio, Bergognone, Luino and Bramantino, along with a large group of Flemish and Dutch works. The rest of the rooms are devoted to later works of art and curios including the gloves that Napoleon wore at Waterloo.

Santa Maria Presso San Satiro

You could easily miss this little jewel, tucked away between four streets south of the Piazza del Duomo (Via Speronari 3; open Mon–Fri 7.30am–11.30am, 3.30–6.30pm, Sat and Sun 9.30am–noon, 3.30–7pm). Legend has it that a fresco of the *Madonna and Child,* which decorated the 9th-century chapel of San Satiro, shed blood when it was vandalised in 1242. Bramante was commissioned to restructure the chapel and provide a safe haven for the fresco, which you can see on the high altar. The architect ingeniously created the impression of depth in the church by the creation of a *trompe l'oeil* apse.

The Cappella della Pietà (off the left transept) has some early medieval frescos and a terracotta *Pietà* scene (1482) by Agosto De Fondutis, and there are more of his terracottas in the lovely baptistery. Bramante's plans for the facade never materialised, the present one being 19th-century neo-Renaissance. The beautiful bell tower at the back of the church, seen from Via Falcone, is one of the oldest in Lombardy.

CASTELLO SFORZESCO & THE NORTHWEST

The monumental Castello Sforzesco was the stronghold and residence of the mighty Milanese dynasties, the Visconti and Sforzas. Dating from 1360 and extended over the centuries, it is the city's largest historical complex, and stands as a symbol of the dramatic events of Milan's history. It is home to no less than five museums, and the works of art within them could keep you busy for an entire day or more. The spacious Parco Sempione, stretching from the castle to the Arco della Pace, was formerly a hunting reserve of the Sforzas; since the late 19th century it has been a public park.

► Castello Sforzesco

The original castle was built in 1360–70 by Galeazzo II Visconti, and was extended by his successor, Gian Galeazzo. Measuring 180m by 180m (590ft by 590ft), with a tower in

An Enduring Logo

A serpent devouring a child is one of the Visconti family symbols, and you can spot it on the frescoed ceilings of the Castello Sforzesco. The derivation remains a mystery. It could represent the dragon which terrorised Milan in the early 5th century and which was slaughtered by Uberto of Angera, founder of the Visconti, or it could reflect the snake talisman that the Lombards used to wear around their necks. You can still see the symbol all round the city – particularly on the Alfa Romeo logo. When Romano Cattaneo, an Alfa draughtsman, was waiting for a tram in Piazza Castello in 1910, he drew inspiration for the logo of the new Milan-based company from the serpent coat of arms embellishing the castle gateway. On the left side of the Alfa Romeo logo is a red cross on a white background, symbol of Milan.

each of the four corners, this was a vast, oppressive fortification with drawbridges over a deep moat, connecting to an outer wall (the Ghirlanda). In 1447 the Visconti fell from power and the townsfolk tore down the fortifications, using the old stones to pay off debts and restore the old town walls.

Under the next ruling dynasty, the Sforzas, the castle was transformed into the Corte Ducale, a sumptuous ducal residence. Beside it they constructed the **Cortile della Rocchetta** – a fort within a fort – and added the lofty Torre di Bona (Bona Tower). During this golden age in Milan's history, leading literati, artists and musicians were summoned to the court. In the late 15th century, Leonardo da Vinci was nominated engineer and painter to the Court and Donato Bramante was enlisted as a court architect and painter.

Imposing Castello Sforzesco

In 1497 Louis XII of France claimed his right to the duchy of Milan, and the last of the Sforzas fled into exile. Under the Spaniards the castle was used purely for military purposes; and after the French attacked the city in 1733 it fell into decline. Napoleon Bonaparte restored what was left of it for military use, creating a spacious parade ground, transforming the ducal chapel into stables and turning the ducal apartments into dormitories.

> Visitors can purchase a well-priced three-day ticket to cover entrance to the castle museums, plus the Natural History, Archaeological and Risorgimento museums. The castle opens daily 9am–7pm, 6pm in winter (free of charge); its museums Tues–Sun 9am–5.30pm, admission fee except on Fri 2–5.30pm, Tues–Thur and on weekends 4.30–5.30pm; <www.milanocastello.it>. To view the battlements call 02 6596937.

Plans to demolish the castle in the late 19th century were thwarted by the architect Luca Beltrami, who, in 1893–1904, restored its aspect as a Renaissance fortress and created a major museum complex within its walls *(see left)*.

Heralding the castle from the city side is the eyecatching 'bundle of rods' fountain, a 1999 reconstruction of the original which was built in 1930 by the Fascists. The Milanese nickname the fountain *'tort de' spus'*, the local dialect for 'wedding cake'. Start your visit at the **Torre del Filarete** (Filarete Tower), which faces the city. Built in 1452 by the Florentine Antonio Averlino and familiarly known as 'Il Filarete', the tower collapsed when gunpowder stored here exploded in 1521. The tower you see today is an early 20th-century reconstruction. The gateway leads into the huge courtyard, the Piazza d'Armi (currently under restoration), and from here to the Corte Ducale, where the Sforzas resided.

Castle Museums

The **Raccolte d'Arte Antica** (Museum of Ancient Art) occupies 12 rooms on the ground floor of the Corte Ducale and contains an extensive collection of sculpture, from early Christian through medieval to the Renaissance. Exhibits include a late Roman sarcophagus, Romanesque sculpture and Bonino da Campione's hard-to-miss equestrian Mausoleum of Bernabò Visconti, who ruled Milan from 1354–1385. The vault of the Sale delle Asse (Room 8) is frescoed with a complex mass of laurel branches, designed by Leonardo da Vinci and executed by pupils – though much restored.

The two most famous pieces in the entire castle collection are reserved for the last room of the Ancient Art Museum (No. 15). Hidden away behind a grey partition wall is Michelangelo's ***Rondanini Pietà*** (1554–64). This evocative sculptural group was left unfinished – Michelangelo was working on it for nine years and up to just days before his death (aged 88). The work went through at least two different stages, and you can still identify parts of the original, most notably Christ's hanging right arm. The other masterpiece is Agostini Busto's **tomb of Gaston de Foix**, the young commander of the French army who fell heroically at Ravenna in 1512.

The upper floor in the Ducal Court houses the **Raccolta dei Mobili** (Museum of Furniture), which has a collection that ranges from 15th-century antiques to contemporary pieces of the 21st century, and the **Pinacoteca** (Art Gallery), which has 230 works of art from the medieval era to the

View to the Duomo from the Castello Sforzesco

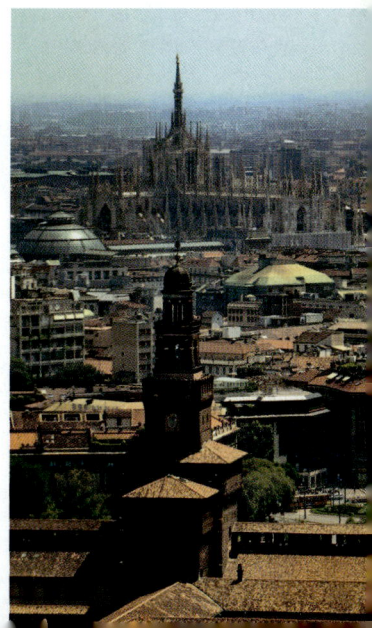

18th century. These are mostly by Lombard artists, but there are also works by Venetian masters, including Mantegna, Giovanni Bellini and Tintoretto.

Further exhibits are arranged around the porticoed Cortile della Rocchetta, which is accessed via the staircase near the ticket office. The first and second floors house the **Museo degli Strumenti Musicali** (Museum of Musical Instruments) and the **Civiche Raccolte d'Arte Applicata** (Collection of Applied Arts) respectively. Room No. 37, the Sala della Balla, houses the rare Trivulzio Tapestries, which were designed by Bramantino and represent the months of the year.

If by now you are not suffering from cultural overload, make your way to the basement of the Cortile della Rocchetta to see the Egyptian and prehistoric collections of the **Archaeological Museum**.

Enjoying Castello Sforzesco's 'wedding cake' fountain

Parco Sempione

Stretching out behind the Castello Sforzesco is the Parco Sempione. The Sforzas created a hunting ground here which was six times the size of the present park. Napoleon had grand plans to build a new and monumental city focusing on the park, but only got as far as the Arena and the **Arco della Pace** (Arch of Peace).

Arco della Pace

Built at the northwest end of the park, this classical triumphal arch marked the start of the route to the Simplon Pass and France. It was originally named the Arch of Victories and decorated with bas-reliefs commemorating Napoleon's conquests, but work stopped with Napoleon's defeat at Waterloo in 1815 and it was another 24 years before it was completed. The Austrian emperor Francis I switched round the Chariot of Peace on top of the arch to face the centre of Milan (rather than Paris), changed the bas-reliefs and renamed the monument Arch of Peace in commemoration of the 1815 Congress of Vienna.

On the eastern side of the park, the **Arena Civica**, a Roman-style amphitheatre, was the venue of chariot races, festivities and even mock naval battles, using water from the canals. Seating 30,000, it is used today as a sports stadium and a venue for pop concerts and civil weddings.

The park was landscaped in 1893 in the fashionable English style. Extending 47 hectares (116 acres), it's a pleasant enough place by day, with lawns and a lake, cycle paths and children's play areas, but at night it's best avoided.

On the west side, the **Triennale**, or **Palazzo dell'Arte** (<www.triennale.it>), was opened in 1932 as the permanent museum for the triennial exhibition of decorative arts. This has played a key role in national and international debate on architecture and design, and is due to become a museum of design in the near future. Outstanding exhibitions are held here, as well as lectures and seminars. In and around the Triennale are some of Milan's trendiest cafés, serving cocktails and Sunday brunches to the arts crowd.

Close to the Triennale, the metallic **Torre Branca** (Branca Tower) is Milan's answer to the Eiffel Tower (open Wed 10.30am–12.30pm, 4–6.30pm, Fri 2.30–6pm, Sat and Sun 10.30am–2pm, 2.30–7.30pm, and also at night from Tues–Sun 9.30pm–1am; admission fee). Designed in 1933 by the Milanese architect Giò Ponti, the tower closed in 1972 for restoration and finally reopened in 2003. A lift whisks you up 108m (354ft) for a 360-degree panorama of the city. Regrettably, there is no longer a restaurant at the top (it was closed for safety reasons) but, back at the bottom, you can treat yourself to a cocktail and watch the celebrities at the ultra-chic **Just Cavalli Café**. Owned by the fashion designer Robert Cavalli, it is also a hugely overpriced restaurant serving international cuisine.

On the eastern edge of the park near the arena, a small **aquarium** occupies a fine Art Nouveau building decorated with majolica marine scenes and bas-reliefs. The 50 or so tanks contain fish from both temperate and exotic zones.

Monument to Bianchini, Cimitero Monumentale

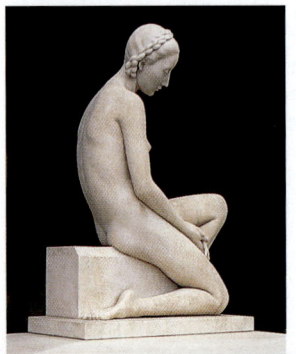

Cimitero Monumentale

Flamboyant tombs and monuments provide a truly fascinating open-air gallery at Milan's **Cimitero Monumentale** (Piazzale Cimitero Monumentale; open Tues–Fri 8.30am–5.15pm, Sat and Sun 8.30am–5.45pm). It lies north of Parco Sempione, close to Stazione Porta Garibaldi, and spreads over 25 hectares (62 acres).

Begun in 1866 and extended over the years, the cemetery is full of Art Nouveau, neoclassical and modern monuments. The focal point is the Famae Aedes (House of Fame), the resting place of various illustrious Italians such as the conductor Arturo Toscanini, the novelist Alessandro Manzoni and the poet Salvatore Quasimodo. You can pick up an informative leaflet in English at the entrance showing the locations of the most famous monuments. Guided tours, in Italian only, take place at 10.15am, advance bookings only (tel: 02 88465600).

The Cimitero Monumentale's elaborate entrance house

Across the railway tracks of Stazione Porta Garibaldi to the east of the cemetery lies **Isola**, Milan's latest up-and-coming neighbourhood. This was formerly a very run-down quarter, but artisans have been setting up workshops here, and it's popular among the young for the newly opened hip bars and cafés.

THE BRERA

A short walk north of La Scala brings you to the Brera, formerly the bohemian quarter of the city. Today, this is a rather chic and picturesque area of narrow cobbled streets, boutiques and trendy nightspots; however, the art galleries and alternative bars still provide a colourful hint of Bohemia. After dark this is a lively quarter. Dozens of nightspots have sprung up, from simple bars where you can sip an *aperitivo* alfresco and tuck into delicious *stuzzichinni* (nibbles) to glitzy nightclubs open until the small hours.

Pinacoteca di Brera

The quarter is home to the Accademia di Belle Arti (Academy of Fine Arts) and the **Pinacoteca di Brera** (Brera Art Gallery, Via Brera 28; open Tues–Sun 8.30am–7.15pm, last entry 6.40pm; admission fee; <www.brera.beniculturali.it>), Milan's showcase museum in the Palazzo Brera, which has one of the finest collections of Italian masterpieces. The Jesuits established a college, library and astronomical observatory here, but when the Order was disbanded in 1772, Empress Maria Theresa of Austria extended the buildings and established the Accademia di Belle Arti. From the nucleus of a handful of paintings, drawings and plastercasts used by students, the collection was expanded with works of art from churches and convents throughout northern Italy that had been suppressed by Napoleon. To these were added examples of art movements from abroad to offer as wide a range as possible.

A bronze statue of Napoleon dressed as a Roman hero greets you as you enter the inner courtyard, where a double stairway leads up to the art galleries. The collection spans some six centuries, and the rooms are roughly chronological (a notable exception is the modern Jesi collection in Room 10). There are 38 rooms, and to do the collection justice you really need two or three visits, or you could break up one long visit with a leisurely lunch in the Brera.

The following is a selection of the many masterpieces on display. *Dead Christ* (*c.*1500) by Mantegna (Room VI) demonstrates the artist's controlled style and mastery of dramatic foreshortening. It was painted at the end of his life and probably intended for his own tomb in the church of Sant'Andrea in Mantua. In the same room there are two notable works by his brother-in-law, Giovanni Bellini: the *Pietà* and a beautiful *Madonna and Child*, painted when he was nearly 80. Room VII has portraits by some of the great Venetian masters; Room VIII has the huge detailed depiction of *St Mark Preaching in Alexandria* begun by Gentile Bellini in 1504 and completed after his death by his brother Giovanni in 1507. Room IX's *Discovery of the Body of St Mark* (1565) by Tintoretto shows the artist's mastery of perspective and

Napoleon stands aloft in the courtyard of the Pinacoteca di Brera

Francesco Hayez's *The Kiss*

theatrical effects of light and movement. In the same room, Veronese's *Feast in the House of Simon* (1570) was originally commissioned as *The Last Supper*, but the hedonistic detail was not appreciated and Veronese found himself before the Inquisition. Room X jumps to the 20th century, with the Jesi private collection of paintings and sculpture, including works by Modigliani Picasso and Braque. In Room XIX the *Madonna of the Rose Garden*, by the prolific Milanese painter, Bernardino Luini, shows the influence of Leonardo da Vinci in his subjects' faces and expressions. Room XXIV has the two most celebrated works in the collection: *The Montefeltro Altarpiece* (1472–4) by Piero della Francesca was painted for his patron, Duke Federico da Montefeltro, who is shown kneeling – the ostrich egg dangling above the Madonna is a famous detail, giving depth to the scene as well as symbolic value (Immaculate Conception); and Raphael's poetic and serene *Marriage of the Virgin* (1504) evokes a sense of harmony between the architecture and the natural world. In Room XXIX *Supper at Emmaus* (1606) by Caravaggio is a fine example of the artist's realism and chiaroscuro; Francesco Hayez's *The Kiss* (1859) in Room XXXVII became a symbol of 19th-century romantic painting.

Churches of the Brera

The loveliest church in the Brera and with the oldest foundations is the Romanesque basilica of **San Simpliciano** (Piazza San Simpliciano; open daily 7am–noon, 3.30–7pm). Thought to have been founded by Sant'Ambrogio in the fourth century, it was reconstructed 800 years later but – apart from the apse and facade, added in 1870 – retains its original Early Christian form. The apse has a fresco of *The Coronation of the Virgin* by the Lombard Renaissance painter Il Bergognone.

San Marco (Piazza San Marco; open daily 8am–noon, 4–7pm) is the largest church after the Duomo. It was dedicated to St Mark, patron saint of Venice, in gratitude to the Venetians for their part in the Lombard League which saw off Frederick Barbarossa, the Holy Roman Emperor, when he laid siege to the city in 1162. Apart from the portal and tower, little is left of the original 13th-century structure: a baroque interior with nine decorated chapels lies behind a neo-Gothic facade.

Overlooking the cobbled Piazza del Carmine, the church of **Santa Maria del Carmine** (open daily 7.30am–noon, 4–7pm) was founded in 1400, rebuilt in Gothic style in 1456 and given a mock Gothic-Lombard facade in 1880. The spacious interior has baroque decoration and many works of art by Camillo Procaccini and Fiammenghino. The pillars at the entrance lean at an alarming angle, due to subsidence. In the adjoining cloister are remains of Roman and medieval sculptural fragments, some of them from funerary monuments, which were once inside the church.

Statue outside the church of Santa Maria del Carmine

NORTHEAST OF THE DUOMO

For most visitors to Milan the main attraction of this quarter of the city will be the exclusive fashion district known as the Quadrilatero d'Oro or the Quadrilatero della Moda. For those who prefer sightseeing, there are art and history museums, including the outstanding collection of paintings and antiques in the Museo Poldi Pezzoli. Further north the Giardini Pubblici (Public Gardens) make a welcome break from the hot city streets in summer.

▶ Quadrilatero d'Oro

Fashion-followers will want to make a beeline for the cutting-edge collections in this world-famous shopping quarter. Easily covered on foot, it is a small, attractive area, bordered by Via Montenapoleone (familiarly known as Montenapo), Via Manzoni, Via Spiga and Via Sant'Andrea. All the big names are here, from Armani, Gucci and Prada to Versace and Dolce & Gabbana. Prices are sky-high, but it's worth coming just to window-shop at the gallery-like boutiques – and see the impeccably clad Milanese who frequent them. Stores range from chic little shops in beautifully preserved *palazzi* to large and modern fashion emporiums. You can take a break from shopping at the historic Café Cova at Via Montenapoleone 8, which offers a mouth-watering selection of cakes; or you can join the fashion crowd at the Armani café or Nobu sushi bar in Armani's megastore at Via Pisoni 1.

Á la mode

Keeping up appearances in the Quadrilatero d'Oro

Museo Bagatti Valsecchi

In the heart of the Quadrilatero d'Oro, the **Museo Bagatti Valsecchi** (Via Gèsu 5; open Tues–Sun 1pm–5.45pm; admission fee; <www.museobagattivalsecchi.org>) is a fascinating museum housed within a neo-Renaissance palace. Brothers Fausto and Giuseppe Valsecchi, following the *fin de siècle* fashion for collecting in 1876–95, transformed two palaces in the style of the mid-1500s, creating an authentic Renaissance atmosphere. The brothers lived here in private apartments but shared the drawing room, dining room and gallery of armour.

Every work of art, furnishing and tapestry is either an original Renaissance piece or a perfect copy. Rooms have been lavishly decorated with painted ceilings, frescos, tapestries and elaborate fireplaces, while 19th-century necessities such as the bathtub are cleverly masked in a Renaissance-style marble niche.

Museo Poldi Pezzoli

Via Manzoni is lined by noble *palazzi*, and one not to be missed is No. 12, home to the **Museo Poldi Pezzoli** (open Tues–Sat 10am–6pm; admission fee; <www.museopoldipezzoli.it>). Gian Giacomo Poldi Pezzoli, who owned the palace, certainly had good taste – it contains an exquisite collection of art, antiques and curios. With an inherited fortune and the assistance of leading artists, craftsmen and connoisseurs, Poldi Pezzoli restored the palace and filled it with his priceless works of art. He stipulated that on his death the building and contents should be accessible to the public. The museum opened in 1881, with the Arms and Armoury (Poldi Pezzoli's great passion) forming the nucleus of the collec-

Grand Hotel et de Milan

The Grand Hotel et de Milan at Via Manzoni 29 opened in 1863 as the Albergo di Milano. Towards the end of the 19th century, it was the only hotel in the city that offered post and telegraph services, and hence was popular with diplomats and businessmen. A stone's throw from La Scala, it has long been a favourite among musicians and artists. The Italian composer Giuseppe Verdi (1813–1901) stayed here from 1872 until his death, with breaks at his country residence in Sant' Agata, near Parma.

After an absence of 24 years from La Scala he made his comeback with a performance of *Otello* in 1887. Afterwards, the Milanese hailed the composer, gathering below his balcony at the Albergo, and he sung an encore of the opera's arias with the tenor Tamagno. In the last years of Verdi's life, frequent bulletins about his health were posted in the hotel lobby, and whenever he was seriously ill crowds would gather outside. During his dying hours the Via Manzoni was laid out with straw to muffle the clatter of the carriages. Other eminent guests at the hotel include kings, emperors, presidents, famous artists and film stars.

tion. To this was added 15th–18th-century Italian paintings, sculpture, Persian carpets, porcelain and Murano glass. The highlights are paintings by Renaissance masters in the Salone Dorato (Golden Salon), such as Mantegna's *Portrait of a Man* and *Madonna and Child,* Piero della Francesca's *Deposition* and *St Nicholas of Tolentino* and Botticelli's *Madonna and Child.* But the favourite painting and the one that has become the logo of the museum is the enchanting *Portrait of a Young Woman* by Piero del Pollaiuolo (1441–96).

Portrait of a Young Woman at Museo Poldi Pezzoli

History Museums

For serious sightseers, and particularly those with an interest in Italian history, there are three museums about the city in the area. At Via Sant'Andrea 6, the Palazzo Morando Attendolo Bolognini is home to the restored **Museo di Milano** (open Tues–Fri 2–5.30pm; free), a fine example of an 18th-century aristocratic residence, with period furnishings and paintings, prints and documents relating to historical events of the 18th and 19th centuries. Sharing the palace is the **Museo di Storia Contemporanea** (Museum of Contemporary History; open Tues–Sun 10am–6pm; free) covering the period 1914–45, but currently only open for temporary exhibitions. The **Museo del Risorgimento** in Palazzo Moriggia, Via Borgonuovo 23 (open Tues–Sun 9am–1pm, 2–5.30pm; admission fee, *see page 42*) traces Italian history leading up to Unification.

Giardini Pubblici

Via Manzoni leads up to the Porta Nuova, the last surviving gateway of the medieval walls. Across Piazza Cavour the **Giardini Pubblici** (Public Gardens) were originally designed by Piermarini in 1782, then extended and redesigned in the 19th century in English style. At the near end of the park, the imposing **Villa Reale** (Royal Villa) has undergone a revamp and been renamed Villa Belgiojoso Bonaparte after the counts of Barbiano di Belgiojoso, for whom it was built, and the French emperor, who lived here with Josephine.

Today, the villa belongs to the City of Milan and is home to the **Civica Galleria d'Arte Moderna** (Civic Gallery of Modern Art; open Tues–Sun 9am–1pm, 2–5.30pm; free). The grandiose neoclassical rooms make a fine setting for the large collection of 19th–20th century works of art, but there is a frustrating lack of information. Worth a special mention are the bronze and gesso sculptures by the 20th-century Italian sculptor Marino Marini (1901–80), including busts of his famous friends in the art world. The villa gardens, with lawns, a fish-filled lake and Doric temple, are open to the public and offer a more secluded setting than the Giardini Pubblici.

The **Padiglione d'Arte Contemporanea** (Pavilion of Contemporary Art) was built beside the Villa Reale as an exhibition space for contemporary art shows in the 1950s. Devastated by a Mafia car bomb in 1993, the pavilion was reconstructed according to its original design. (To find out what's on, visit <www.comune.milano.it/pac>.)

On the west side of the park, the Palazzo Dugnani houses the little **Museo del Cinema** (open Fri–Sun 3–6pm; admission fee), packed with antique viewing contraptions and movie memorabilia. On the opposite side, the **Museo Civico di Storia Naturale** (Natural History Museum, Corso Venezia 55; open Tues–Fri 9.30am–6pm, Sat and Sun 9.30am–6.30pm; admission fee, *see page 42*) is the biggest of its kind in Italy. It has reconstructions of dinosaurs and striking dioramas as well as specialist sections such as geology, mineralogy, palaeontology and entomology.

The nearby **Planetario 'Ulrico Hoepli'** (Ulrico Hoepli Planetarium, Corso Venezia 57; open Mon–Fri 9am–noon; admission fee; <www.comune.milano.it/planetario> in Italian only) was donated to the city by the publisher Ulrico Hoepli. There are shows on Tuesday and Thursday evenings and weekend afternoons; for details visit their website.

Corso Venezia, the traffic-clogged artery bordering the Giardini on the southeast, is not very conducive to sightseeing, but it is overlooked by some of the city's finest neoclassical palaces. The splendid **Palazzo Rocca-Saporiti** at No. 40 (1812) is topped by 12 Roman gods and decorated with a frieze depicting scenes from Milanese history. Going south, on the Giardini side, the monumental **Palazzo Castiglioni** at

The Planetario 'Ulrico Hoepli' in the Giardini Pubblici

No. 47 is nicknamed Ca' di Ciapp (House of the Buttocks) after the female nudes which used to decorate the portal. The vast **Palazzo Serbelloni** at No. 16 was a residence of Napoleon and Josephine, King Vittorio Emanuele II and other eminent figures in Milanese history. It was badly damaged in World War II, but you can still see some of the frescos in the loggia. The **Casa Fontana-Silvestri** at No. 10 is one of Milan's few Renaissance palaces, and the finest along the Corso. It was built in the late 15th century.

WEST OF CENTRE

Leonardo's *The Last Supper* is the star attraction of this section of the city, but it is also home to the great basilica of Sant'Ambrogio, a favourite church of the Milanese, the city's archaeology museum and the largest science and technology museum in Italy. A religious quarter in medieval days with at least 10 monasteries, today it is an affluent 19th-and 20th-century residential district, with some fine *palazzi* and prestigious shops on the Corso Magenta, as well as a few very pleasant hotels with easy access to the centre.

➤ The Last Supper

In *A Traveller in Italy* (1964) H.V. Morton commented that 'there can be few cities in the world, in which you can give the title of a great picture as a topographical direction'. He was referring to Leonardo da Vinci's ***The Last Supper*** (*Il Cenacolo*) and the fact that the name of the painting is all he had to say to the Milan taxi driver to get him there. Thanks to Dan Brown's best-selling novel, and the film, *The Da Vinci Code*, visitor numbers to this celebrated masterpiece are higher than ever. Bookings are taken weeks in advance, and those who arrive on spec are usually turned away *(see page 60)*.

Commissioned in 1495 by Ludovico il Moro for the Dominican convent of Santa Maria delle Grazie, *The Last Supper*

Leonardo's *The Last Supper* – queues to see it are weeks long

covers the whole width of the refectory north wall. It is a vast and dramatic mural, and despite heavy restoration and repainting over the centuries, seeing it is a moving and strangely compelling experience. A masterpiece of psychological insight, the work shows the emotional reactions on the faces of the Apostles at the split second they hear Christ's announcement that one of them is about to betray him. Their expressions of amazement and disbelief, and the motion depicted by their faces and gestures, contrast with the divine stillness of the central figure of Christ. The only figure to recoil and the only one whose face is not in the light is Judas, the third figure to the left of Christ.

Restoration works, good and bad, have been hampered by Leonardo's experimental technique in painting in *tempera forte*, rather than *fresco* – he applied the paint to dry plaster rather than applying it quickly to a wet surface. This gave him more time to complete the work, but meant that the moisture caused the paint to flake. On completion in 1498, the work drew high praise, but even in Leonardo's lifetime the work had begun to disintegrate. When the art historian Vasari saw it a generation later he described it as 'a dazzling blotch'. Reworked in the 18th century, the painting was then badly damaged during the Napoleonic regime when the premises became a stable and the wall was used for target practice. In the following century, heavy-handed restorers managed to peel off an entire layer. Miraculously, the work survived the bombs that fell on the building in 1943. A long and painstaking restoration process took place in 1978–99, giving rise to major controversy in the art world. Many ex-

Visiting *The Last Supper*

Tickets for *The Last Supper* can only be booked in advance, either via the call centre, with a lot of patience – and money, if you are calling from abroad – on 02 89421146 (Mon–Fri 9am–6pm, Sat 9am–2pm) or, theoretically, online at <www.cenacolovinciano.org>. However, at the time of writing, the system was experiencing major problems. Large numbers of tickets are allocated to tour operators and agents, some of which are sold online, with a hefty booking fee. Alternatively, you could take the expensive three-hour morning city sightseeing coach tour (<www.autostradale.com>) which departs from the Piazza del Duomo; but you still have to book in advance and a guarantee of seeing the painting is only assured on certain (unpredictable) days.

The painting is in the refectory of the Convent of Santa Maria delle Grazie (Piazza Santa Maria delle Grazie; open 8.15am–6.45pm), which is kept at a precise temperature and humidity. A maximum of 25 visitors at a time have to pass through three acclimatisation and depolluting chambers before gaining access, and visits are restricted to 15 minutes. Audio guides are available in five languages, and there are guided tours in English on Tues–Sun at 9.30am and 3.30pm.

perts consider the restored colours far too bright.

On the facing wall, *The Crucifixion* (1495) by Donato da Montorfano gets short shrift, especially as the time in the refectory is restricted to 15 minutes. But this is also of interest to Leonardo fans, for he added the (now faded) portraits of Ludovico il Moro, the Sforza ruler, with his wife Beatrice and their children, to the painting.

Santa Maria delle Grazie

Such is the fame of *The Last Supper*, that the convent church of **Santa Maria delle Grazie** is often overlooked. This is a lovely Gothic/Renaissance church (open Mon–Sat 7am–noon, 3–7pm, Sun 7.30am–12.15pm, 3.30–9pm) with a magnificent brick-and-terracotta exterior, a grandiose dome and delightful cloisters. The church was built by Guiniforte Solari in Gothic style, but shortly afterwards Ludovico il Moro commissioned Bramante to demolish the chancel and rebuild it as a Renaissance mausoleum for himself and his wife, Beatrice d'Este. His plans for further building were dashed by the French occupation in 1499, and so the interior feels like two different churches: Solari's original with richly decorated arches and vaults, and beyond it Bramante's pure, perfect and simple Renaissance cube, with a massive dome.

Santa Maria delle Grazie

Leonardo da Vinci's 'Vitruvian Man' drawing

Science Museum

For further proof of Leonardo's genius visit the **Museo Nazionale della Scienza e della Tecnologia Leonardo da Vinci** (Museum of Science and Technology, Via San Vittore 21; open Tues–Fri 9.30am–5pm, Sat–Sun 9.30am–6.30pm; admission fee), south of the church of Santa Maria delle Grazie. This is a massive and somewhat daunting museum, which has been set within the cloisters and ancient remains of the monastery of St Vittore and other buildings that were added later.

Exhibits numbering over 10,000 cover all the sciences, and include displays as diverse as arts and crafts, watchmaking, hammer-forging, locomotion and the workings of the internet. The latest addition is the Enrico Toti submarine, which in 2005 was towed from the Adriatic up the River Po to Cremona, carted on wheels, and over several nights inched its way through the streets of Milan before arriving at the museum.

In the **Leonardo Gallery** (first floor), the collection of models demonstrates the genius of Leonardo's inventions. His technical drawings are reproduced along with modern interpretative drawings and descriptions. Leonardo never intended his designs to be used for construction plans – and in some cases the machines don't work. Not that this detracts from their appeal – some of the machines were developed later with success.

Museo Archeologico and San Maurizio

On the same street as Santa Maria delle Grazie, going towards the centre, is the **Civico Museo Archeologico** (Civic Museum of Archaeology, Corso Magenta 15; open Tues–Sun 9am–1pm, 2–5.30pm; admission fee, but free 4.30–5.30pm and Fri 2–5pm, *see page 42*). Set among the cloisters and ruins of the 15th-century Monastero Maggiore, formerly Milan's largest convent, the museum houses fine examples of Roman sculptures, mosaics, ceramics and glassware. Star exhibits are the gilded silver Parabiago Plate, with engravings of the goddess Cybele, and the Coppa Trivulzio, an emerald-green glass goblet, both dating from the 4th century. Further sections are devoted to Greek, Etruscan, Indian

The Horse That Never Was

In 1482 Ludovico Sforza, duke of Milan, commissioned Leonardo da Vinci to create a 7-m (24-ft) high bronze horse which was to be the largest equine statue ever conceived and Leonardo's most important work. The multi-talented genius, who was busy producing city plans for Milan, a defence system for the castle, additions to the canal network and costumes for ducal entertainments, took years to complete the full-scale clay model. By the time it was finished, war with the French was imminent, and the bronze designated for the monument was cast into cannons. French troops arrived in 1499, and the colossal model was used for target practice by their archers.

In 1999, a bronze replica of the equestrian monument was erected in the new Cultural Park (open daily 9am–6.30pm; <www.leonardoshorse.org>) in San Siro. This suburb of Milan, once fields and orchards, was the designated area for the original bronze. Conceived and cast in the US, the horse was sculpted according to Leonardo's notes and drawings, and was donated to Milan in appreciation 'of the genius of Leonardo and the legacy of the Italian Renaissance'.

and medieval collections. Behind the museum you can see the ruins of a 24-sided Roman tower and a segment of the old town wall.

Beside the Archaeological Museum, and built for the Benedictine nuns from the Monastero Maggiore, is the 16th-century church of **San Maurizio** (open Tues–Sun 9am–1pm, 2.30–5.30pm). The sober grey-stone facade on the street belies a wonderfully decorative frescoed interior. The nuns were cut off from the main congregation by the partition wall, and to the right of the altar you can see the tiny opening through which they received Holy Communion. The church frescos are the work of 16th-century Lombard artists, and most notably those of Bernardino Luini. In the lunettes either side of the altar you can see his portrayals of the donor of the frescos, Alessandro Bentivoglio, prince of Bologna, and his wife Ippolita Sforza.

Frescos in the church of San Maurizio

Basilica di Sant' Ambrogio

One of the city's symbols and arguably its loveliest church, **Sant'Ambrogio** (Piazza Sant' Ambrogio; open daily 7am–noon, 3–7pm) was founded in the 4th century by Ambrogio, the city's bishop and future patron saint *(see page 15)*. The church which you see today – a fine red-brick Romanesque basilica flanked by two campaniles – dates from the 9th–12th centuries and became the prototype for many Lombard-Romanesque basilicas. In front of it the perfectly preserved, porticoed **atrium** was built as a shelter for pilgrims. The composite columns here have finely carved capitals, with lively sculptures of mythical creatures and Christian symbols.

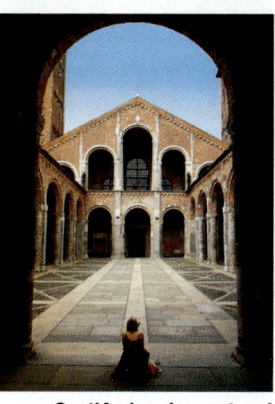

Sant'Ambrogio courtyard

Inside is the beautifully carved Byzantine-Romanesque **pulpit**, standing over a 4th-century Palaeochristian sarcophagus. Below the 9th-century ciborium (canopy) is the jewel-encrusted gold and silver **altarpiece** (835), a masterpiece by the German goldsmith Volvinio. Panels on the front depict scenes from the *Life of Christ*, and on the back the *Life of Sant' Ambrogio*. To the right of the sacristy the **Cappella di San Vittore in Ciel d'Oro** (Chapel of St Victor in the Sky of Gold) is decorated by splendid 5th-century mosaics, depicting Sant' Ambrogio and other saints. In the crypt below the presbytery the saint's remains share a silver-and-crystal urn with those of the martyred Roman soldiers Gervasius and Protasius. Further relics can be seen in the Museo Diocesano *(see page 71)*.

SOUTH MILAN: PORTA TICINESE & NAVIGLI

It is hard to believe that landlocked Milan was once an important port with a major network of canals. Trade on the waterways ceased in the late 1970s, and the Navigli or canal quarter has since been undergoing a transformation. Galleries, trattorias and bars proliferate along the towpaths, and the area is now one of the city hotspots for nightlife. Between the Duomo and the Navigli lie two of Milan's oldest and finest churches, San Lorenzo and Sant'Eustorgio. Further east, the now traffic-clogged Corso di Porta Romana was the ancient road to Rome, and the nearby Ca'Grande one of the largest and most elegant hospitals in Italy.

The Navigli

The Navigli were key navigable waterways, linking Milan to the River Ticino, which descends from Switzerland via Lake Maggiore to Pavia and, via the Po, to the sea. Work on the Naviglio Grande (Grand Canal) started in 1177, and the waterway was initally used by horse- and oxen-drawn barges. The first 30km (19 miles) took half a century and involved hundreds of men with shovel and axe. They finally reached Milan in 1272, but works came to a standstill when the Milanese opposed the project, particularly the clergy who were charged a new tax to help finance it. In 1359, under Galeazzo II Visconti, excavations began on the Naviglio Pavese, the canal to Pavia which was conceived primarily for the irrigation of the great park that had been created for the Visconti castle at Pavia. Under his suc-

> The Cerchia di Navigli was the circle of navigable canals surrounding the city. In 1930, when canal trade was on the decline, the waterways were filled in to become Milan's traffic-clogged ring road.

The Navigli quarter is one of the city's nightlife hotspots

cessor, Gian Galeazzo Visconti, the foundation stone of Milan's Duomo was laid (1386), and the canals then became an invaluable means of transport. Huge blocks of marble from the Candoglia quarries near Lake Maggiore were transported to Milan by barges along the Ticino River and then via the Naviglio Grande to the city dockyard. Leonardo da Vinci was fascinated by the system of waterways, and one of his many tasks during his employment in the court of Ludovico il Moro of the Sforza dynasty was to suggest improvements for the canal network.

Following the Sforza dynasty, long periods of neglect and deterioration were brought about by foreign rule, wars, pestilence and earthquakes. In 1809, under Napoleon, the first section of the Naviglio Pavese became navigable, and in 1816, after 600 years, the 50km (30 miles) of the Naviglio Grande was finally completed. Added to the 101km (63 miles) of other canals and 81km (50 miles) of navigable river reaches, this formed a waterway network of 232km (145 miles). Between 1830 and the end of the century, an annual average of 8,300 barges, transporting 350,000 tonnes of trade, arrived at the dockyard of Porta Ticinese.

Canal traffic suffered with competition from railways in the 19th century, but saw a brief surge of activity during the post-war building boom. In 1953 the dockyard of Porta Ticinese was ranked the 13th-most important port in Italy in terms of trade. But competition from road transport finally led to the demise of canal trade, the waterways were filled in and turned into roads, and the last barge delivered its load of sand at the Darsena in 1979. Nowadays, the only water transport is the new tourist service which offers tours of the few surviving canals (tel: 02 67020288, <www.navigamilano.it>).

Café in the Navigli

The Navigli Today

The **Porta Ticinese** on Piazzale XXIV Maggio heralds the Navigli quarter. This original gateway, which formed part of the 12th-century city walls, was replaced in 1804 by the present-day monumental arch. It stands isolated in the square, surrounded by traffic.

Formerly the most insalubrious quarter of the city, the Navigli has seen major regeneration over the last few decades, and now has a mix of working-class and upwardly mobile residents. The industrial sites and tenement blocks have been made into designer apartments by prosperous young Milanese, towpaths are lined with galleries, antique workshops and quirky shops, giving it a trendy, vaguely bohemian air, while a host of bars, jazz clubs and restaurants ensure a lively nightlife. Dozens of events take place here: festivals and fairs, markets and art exhibitions, concerts and theatre. Apart from the weekly flea market, there is the huge Mercatone dell'Antiquariato on the last Sunday of the month from September to June, with around 400 antique dealers spreading their wares along the banks of the canal.

> **The Associazione del Naviglio Grande** (<www.navigamilano.it>) is running experimental one-hour mini-cruises along the 'Navigli di Leonardo' (Leonardo Canals) from April to September. Boats depart from Alzaia Naviglio 66, or you can book tickets in advance at Alzaia Naviglio Grande 4, tel: 02 89409971.

The **Darsena** (dockyard), built in 1603, used to be the hub of the Navigli quarter, where barges docked to offload their cargo. Today, this is a neglected stretch of murky water, waiting its turn for regeneration. The quarter comes alive on Saturdays when the stalls of the Fiera di Senigallia flea market are spread out along Viale G. D'Annunzio. This was originally part of the dock, but was paved over in the 1980s.

Most of the Navigli action, particularly after dark, takes place along the two towpaths running either side of the Naviglio Grande: the Ripa di Porta Ticinese and the Alzaia del Naviglio Grande. Barges have been converted into bars and restaurants, plus there are nightclubs, jazz clubs, *aperitivo* bars and a host of trattorias with tables set out along the banks of the canals. Come in the daytime, though, and, unless there's a fair or market, it can be rather dull and lifeless.

Many of the restaurants are closed, and although pleasant enough, it is not especially picturesque. The prettiest corner is the **Vicolo del Lavandai** (Laundry Lane), off the Alzaia Naviglio Grande at the Porta Ticinese end. This is named after the old wash-houses, which retain their wooden roofs and the stone slabs where the laundry was scrubbed.

Ancient Basilicas

The two great basilicas of the Ticinese quarter lie just east of the main Corso di Porta Ticinese. **Sant'Eustorgio** (Piazza Sant'Eustorgio; open Mon–Sat 7.30am–noon, 3.30–6.30pm), distinctive for its lofty bell tower, has Early Christian origins, but was destroyed by Frederick Barbarossa in 1162 and rebuilt over several centuries. Highlights of the church are the private Renaissance chapels, and most notably the beautiful little **Cappella Portinari** (1462–6), which can only be seen by visiting the Museo di Sant'Eustorgio (open Tues–Sun 10am–6pm, but closed August and mornings in July; admission fee, combined ticket with Museo Diocesano and the Cappella Sant'Aquilino at San Lorenzo, *see opposite*). Similar to Brunelleschi's Cappella Pazzi in Florence, this simple chapel was one of the first Renaissance works in the city. Traditionally attributed to the Florentine Michelozzo, it is now believed to have been designed by a Lombard architect working in Tuscan circles. The chapel was commissioned by Pigello Portinari, a Florentine nobleman and agent of the Medici Bank in Milan, to house the relics of St Peter Martyr – as

Sant'Eustorgio's domed ceiling

well as his own. St Peter Martyr (or Pietro da Verona) was an Inquisitor who persecuted the Cathars, one of whom took revenge and killed him in 1252. His relics lie in the lavishly carved marble sarcophagus (1339), a masterpiece by Giovanni Balduccio from Pisa. The saint's skull is protected in a silver reliquary in the chapel to the left of the altar. Stunning frescos by the Tuscan artist Vincenzo Foppa decorate the chapel and depict scenes from the *Life of St Peter Martyr* and the *Virgin Mary*.

Lavish marble sarcophagus in the Portinari Chapel

The basilica was built to house the supposed relics of the Magi. These are contained in a Roman sarcophagus in the Chapel of the Magi in the right-hand transept of the main church. During the annual Corteo dei Magi procession on 6 January (Epiphany), the relics are carried with great ceremony from the Duomo to Sant'Eustorgio.

Unlike many diocesan museums which are dull and dusty, Milan's has been renovated and feels like a stylish new art gallery. Beside Sant'Eustorgio, the **Museo Diocesano** (Corso di Porta Ticinese 95; open Tues–Sun 10am–6pm; admission fee: combined ticket option, *see opposite*; <www.museodiocesano.it>) is set out on three floors of the Dominican convent and cloisters, and showcases 320 works

Statue of Constantine

from Sant'Ambrogio *(see page 65)* and other churches in the diocese. The works date from the 6th to the 19th centuries, and, as well as religious paintings, there are sculptures, vestments, holy vessels and jewellery. Several rooms are devoted to the collections of various archbishops of Milan, giving a good idea of their taste in art. Don't miss the Fondi Oro collection – exquisite Tuscan and Umbrian altarpieces, all with a gold background.

A rose-lined path through the Parco delle Basiliche (Park of the Basilicas) links Sant'Eustorgio and San Lorenzo. For many centuries public hangings and torture took place here, while tanners' workshops created a foul stench. Today it is a pleasant park which affords the best views of the **Basilica di San Lorenzo Maggiore** (Corso di Porta Ticinese 39; open daily 7.30am–6.45pm). After the Duomo, this is the second-largest church in the city, distinctive for its huge central dome and the melange of architectural styles. It is also the oldest surviving church of the city, founded in the 4th century as an early Christian church, remodelled in Romanesque form in the 13th century, and reconstructed in the 16th century after the collapse of the dome and part of the walls in 1573. The facade is the newest addition, dating from 1894.

The 16 lofty Corinthian columns on the square in front of the church came from a Roman temple, and were probably erected here as a part of a portico for the original basilica, hence the alternative name for the church, **San Lorenzo alle Colonne**. In front of the church is a 1942 statue of Constantine the Great, who issued the Edict of Milan, granting freedom of religion to Christians in 313, before the church was built.

Inside the church the Early Christian octagonal plan, though remodelled in the 16th century, has essentially been preserved. On the right, the **Cappella Sant'Aquilino** (open daily 9.30am–12.30pm, 2.30–6.30pm; admission fee: combined ticket option, *see page 70*) was built as an imperial mausoleum and retains some beautiful 5th-century niche mosaics. At the altar, an elaborate silver-and-crystal casket contains the remains of Sant'Aquilino. A small stairway to the left of the altar descends to the imperial-era foundations.

Building material for San Lorenzo was thought to have been salvaged from the nearby Roman Circus and Amphitheatre. Remnants of the latter can be seen at the **Parco dell' Anfiteatro** (Amphitheatre Park, inconspicuous entrance at Via de Amicis 17; open Tues–Fri 9am–6pm, 4.30pm winter,

Corinthian columns at the Basilica di San Lorenzo Maggiore

Sat 9am–2pm summer only; free). The remains of this huge four-storey colosseum were discovered during roadworks here in 1931. Within the park, the Antiquarium (open Wed, Fri and Sat 9am–2pm) displays architectural finds from the area, and to liven things up, shows excerpts from *Spartacus* and *Gladiator*. One gladiator, Ubricus, died at the age of 22 having fought 13 times here.

Around the University

Southeast of the Duomo lies the **Ca'Grande** (open Mon–Fri 8am–12.30pm; free), home to the Università Statale (University of Milan). Also known as the Ospedale Maggiore, it was built in the mid-15th century by Francesco Sforza as an orphanage and a hospital for the poor, and for five centuries it was the main hospital of Milan. The earliest part of this colossal complex was designed by the court architect Antonio Averlino (familiarly known as Filarate), but work was to carry on for another four centuries, incorporating a range of styles. Filarate's 15th-century brickwork facade (on the right side) has been preserved, and his courtyards reconstructed. The beautiful main court has an arcade around a garden and a baroque first-floor loggia added in the 17th century. The complex was badly bombed in 1943, but restorations enabled it to become a university in 1952.

> The vast Palazzo di Giustizia (law courts), east of Ca' Grande, was built in the 1930s in typical Fascist style. The building hit the headlines in the early 1990s during the *Mani Pulite* (Clean Hands) investigations, when huge numbers of politicians and financiers were charged with corruption.

Close by, on the main Corso di Porta Romana, is the church of **San Nazaro Maggiore** (open daily 7.30am–noon, 3–6.30pm). This was one of four churches built outside the city walls in 382–6 by Sant'Ambrogio,

Fascist-style facade of the Palazzo di Giustizia

bishop of Milan, to house the relics of Apostles Andrew, John and Thomas. Ten years later, the remains of San Nazaro, discovered close to the church, were also accommodated. The church was rebuilt in the 11th century and has been heavily worked since. To get into the main church you pass through the Cappella Trivulzio, designed by Bramantino in 1512 as a mausoleum for the Trivulzio family of *condottieri* (mercenaries). When Carlo Borromeo, archbishop of Milan, decreed that churches should only accommodate the relics of saints, the bodies of the Trivulzios were removed.

Towering over the buildings to the north is the 28-storey **Torre Velasca** (Velasca Tower), built in 1956–60. The cantilevered upper section harks back to medieval fortifications, as well as a handy way of creating more accommodation. The top block is residential, and the lower part offices. The tower was one of the first to overtake the gilded Madonnina crowning the Duomo *(see page 26)*.

EXCURSIONS FROM MILAN

With excellent road and rail links, Milan makes a good starting point for excursions in the Lombardy region. The lakes and mountains are surprisingly close. By train you can be in Stresa on Lake Maggiore, Como on Lake Como or Bergamo within an hour. For details see the *Berlitz Pocket Guide to the Italian Lakes and Verona*.

The following are some briefer excursions from Milan. The Abbazia di Chiaravalle and Monza are both on the city outskirts; Pavia and its Certosa are a little further from the city, and offer more than enough sightseeing to occupy a whole day's excursion.

Chiaravalle Abbey

In 1135 French Cistercian monks drained the marshland southeast of Milan, transforming it into rich agricultural land, and built the splendid **Abbazia di Chiaravalle** (Chiaravalle Abbey, Via Sant'Arialdo 102, 7km/4 miles southeast of Milan, metro M3 Corvetto, bus No. 77; open Tues–Sun 6am–12.15pm, 2.30–6.30pm; guided tours three times a day). The founder was St Bernard, who was the Abbot of Clairvaux in France (Chiaravalle in Italian), to which the new abbey was affiliated.

The church was rebuilt in 1150–60, altered over the centuries, and disbanded under Napoleon. A lengthy restoration was completed in the early 1950s, and Cistercian monks finally returned to the abbey. A blend of Lombard Romanesque and French Gothic, the church is notable for its beautiful and dominant terracotta-and-marble campanile, internal Renaissance and baroque frescos, as well as its finely carved wooden choir and cloisters. Sadly, Bramante's Chiostro Grande (Great Cloister) was destroyed in 1861 to make way for the railway line.

Pavia

The ancient university town of **Pavia** lies on the banks of the River Ticino, 36km (22 miles) south of Milan. Long ago it was one of the leading cities in Italy, reaching its zenith from the 6th–8th centuries when it was capital of the Lombard kingdom and site of the coronation of the Holy Roman Emperors. During the 14th century, the city was subdued by the Visconti dynasty of Milan who built the great Certosa di Pavia, the Castello Visconteo (Visconti Castle), and founded the city's university, one of the oldest in Europe and noted particularly for law, science and medicine.

Pavia today is a pleasant provincial town of cobbled streets and squares, Romanesque and Gothic churches, feudal towers and *palazzi*. The enormous 19th-century dome of the Renaissance Duomo (closed for restoration) dominates the centre. Amadeo, Leonardo and Bramante were among its

A covered bridge spans the River Ticino at Pavia

architects, but today it is a disappointing hotchpotch of styles. The pile of rubble beside it is all that remains of the medieval tower which collapsed in 1989, killing four people. The town's oldest and finest church is the **Basilica di San Michele**, a masterpiece of Lombard-Romanesque. The church witnessed the coronation of kings here during the Middle Ages, the last being Frederick Barbarossa in 1155. The glorious facade, in mellow sandstone, is decorated with fascinating (but sadly faded) friezes of beasts, birds, mermaids and humans; there are more carvings inside on the columns, which are better-preserved. The austere **Visconti Castle**, a mere shadow of the former ducal residence, contains the Civic Museum, with collections of paintings, sculpture and archaeology.

Quiet street in Pavia

Certosa di Pavia

The great **Certosa** (Carthusian monastery) lies 8km (5 miles) north of Pavia, among fields which were the former hunting ground of the Visconti. One of the most decorative and important monuments in Italy, it was founded in 1396 by Gian Galeazzo Visconti as a mausoleum for himself and his family. However, it was not completed for another 200 years. The Carthusian Order was suppressed in 1782, and since then the monastery has had a chequered history, closed for long periods or variously occupied by Cistercian, Carmelite and Carthusian monks. In 1866 it was declared a national monument, and since 1968 a small community of monks, this time Cistercian, have occupied the Certosa. Tours, given by one of the monks, are in Italian only, but this is the only way you will get to see the two sets of cloisters and the refectory.

Creating a striking impact as you enter the gateway is

Encrusted facade of the Certosa

the multicoloured marble facade, encrusted with a proliferation of medallions, bas-reliefs and statues of saints and prophets. The monument marks the transition from late Gothic to Renaissance: the interior is essentially Gothic in design, created by some of the same architects and artisans who worked on Milan's Duomo; the lower level of the facade dates from the 15th century, and the plainer upper facade from the first decades of the 16th century.

The soaring interior is a treasure house of Renaissance and baroque works of art. Outstanding among them are the funerary monument of Ludovico il Moro and his wife Beatrice d'Este (though neither is actually buried here), the mausoleum of Gian Galeazzo Visconti, frescos by Bergognone in the transept, chapels and roof vaults, the marquetry in the choir stalls, the altarpiece by Perugino and the Florentine triptych, made of hippopotamus teeth and other animal bones, in the Old Sacristy. Guided tours take in the delightful Small Cloister with terracotta decoration and garden, the

Stained-glass window in Monza's Duomo

refectory and the Great Cloister, lined by 24 monks' dwellings, each complete with chapel, garden, bedroom, study, prayer room and hatch for food deliveries. Visits end at the Certosa shop selling the local Carnaroli rice, honey, herbal remedies and liqueurs (but not, as you might assume, made by the monks).

Regular trains and buses link Pavia with Milan. The Certosa, 8km (5 miles) to the north, has its own train station and bus stop, but both are a 1.5-km (1-mile) walk from the monument, mostly along a main road which can be tiring on a hot summer's day. The Certosa (tel: 0382 925613) is open May–Oct Tues–Sun 9–11.30am and 2.30–6pm, Apr and Sept to 5.30pm, Oct and Mar to 5pm, closed Mon except hols; for guided tours, arrive one hour before closing time. There is no admission fee, but you are expected to give a donation.

Monza

Once an important medieval town and the site of the coronation of many Lombard kings, Monza today merges with the industrial suburbs of northwest Milan and is best-known for Grand Prix motor-racing. The cultural highlight of the town is the Gothic **Duomo di San Giovanni** (Cathedral of St John), founded by the Lombard queen Theodolinda in 595 and rebuilt from the 13th–14th centuries. The Cappella di Teodolinda (Theodolinda Chapel), frescoed with scenes from the life of the queen, contains a sarcophagus with her remains and the gem-studded 'Iron Crown', which was used for the coronation of 34

Lombard kings, from medieval times to the 19th century. The last was Ferdinand I of Austria in 1836, while the penultimate was Napoleon, who assumed the throne of Italy in Milan's cathedral in 1805. Legend has it that a nail within the crown came from Christ's cross – hence the name 'Iron Crown'. Theodolinda-related treasures are kept in the cathedral museum, **Museo Serpero**, including her own bejewelled crown.

Monza's motor-racing takes place in the 800-hectare (1,977-acre) **Parco di Monza**, as do golf, tennis, swimming, bike-hire and other sports and recreations. This was originally the park of the **Villa Reale** (Royal Villa; closed for restoration until 2008), a grand neoclassical villa built in 1777 for Archduke Ferdinand of Austria.

Monza is 15km (9 miles) northeast of Milan, and is linked by a regular timetable of trains from Milan's Stazione Garibaldi or Stazione Centrale.

Monza's Villa Reale, surrounded by a huge park

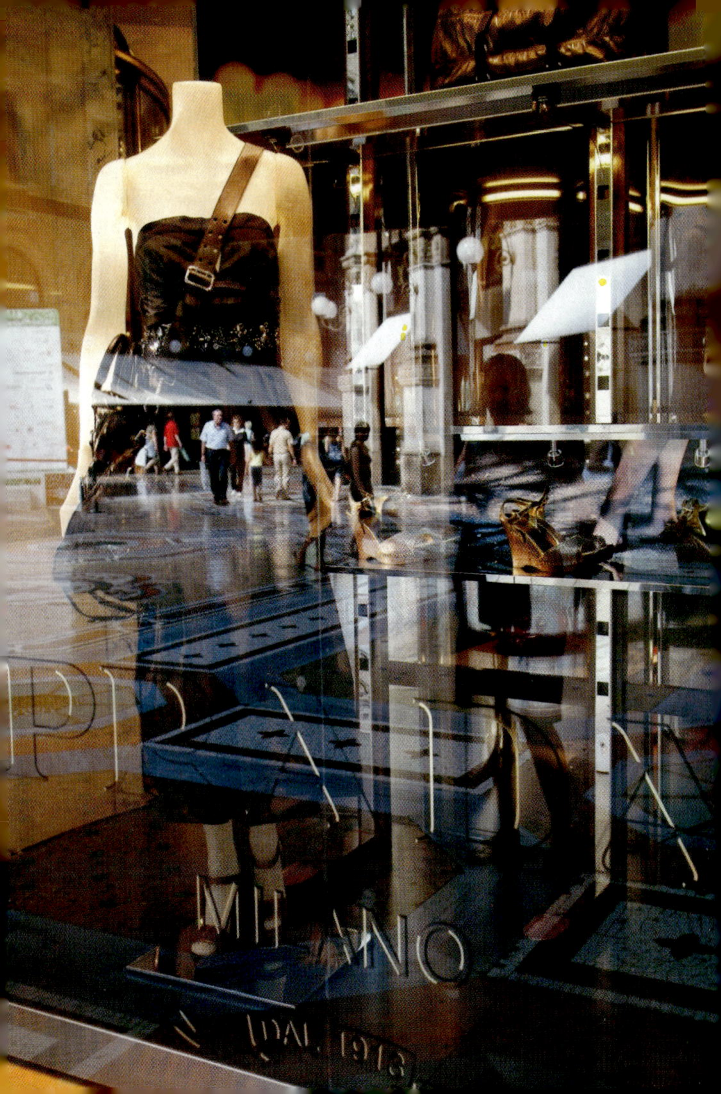
DAL 1913

WHAT TO DO

SHOPPING

The fashion capital of Italy, Milan is a shopper's paradise. Famous for designer boutiques with cutting-edge collections, the city also offers a wide range of more affordable fashions, including vintage and alternative clothing, funky accessories and jewellery, as well as stylish design products and homeware, exotic ethnic items and wonderful food stores.

Fashion and Accessories

The flagship outlets of Armani, Prada, Dolce & Gabbana, Missoni, Versace and many more Italian and international fashion designers are conveniently concentrated in a small and picturesque area known as the Quadrilatero d'Oro. This 'Golden Rectangle', only a short distance from the Duomo, is defined by Via Manzoni, Via Monte Napoleone, Via della Spiga and Via Sant'Andrea. It is also the quarter of Milan's most famous jewellers. The Via Monte Napoleone, where you can find Cartier, Damiani and Buccellati, has been home to jewellers since the 1930s; Tiffany and Bulgari can be found in Via della Spiga.

Stores range from chic little shops in beautifully preserved *palazzi* to large and modern fashion emporiums. Armani has a trendy megastore at Via Manzoni 31 (<www.armani-via manzoni31.com>) with a Nobu sushi bar, café, Sony store, flowers, fine chocolates and books as well as Emporio Armani, Armani Jeans and Armani Casa; on Via Sant'Andrea, Gianfranco Ferré's fashion boutique comes with a spa.

Along the fashionable Corso Como, a Fiat garage has been transformed into the vast and hugely popular fashion

Prada boutique in the Galleria

emporium Corso Como 10 (named after its address). With a tea garden, lounge bar and restaurant, bookshop, art gallery and music shop, you could spend all day here – and since it has three designer suites above the shop, all night too!

More affordable fashions can be found in the chain stores and boutiques in and around the centre of town. Leading off Piazza del Duomo, the Corso Vittorio Emanuele II is lined with high-street stores and boutiques. Northeast from the Giardini Pubblici, Corso Buenos Aires is the longest shopping street in Italy, packed with clothes and shoe shops, chain stores and discounted outlets.

Most of the factory outlets, which offer 20–75 percent off recommended retail prices, are dispersed in the suburbs of the city. If you have time, head for the Armani outlet (Via Provinciale per Bregnano 13, Vertemate con Minobrio; open Tues–Sun; tel: 031 887373), which has some great bargains in its three-storeyed warehouse. Get there by train from Milan's Stazione Cadorna to Fine Mornasco, then a taxi to the outlet – worth it, perhaps, for the discounts of up to 50 percent. Closer to the centre, the Salvagente outlet (Via Bronzetti 16; open Tues–Sat; tel: 02 76110328; <www.salvagentemilano.it>) stocks heavily discounted fashions and accessories from Prada, Armani and other big names.

The Brera, traditionally the bohemian quarter, has some young offbeat boutiques, arts and crafts, and the Navigli, particularly Corso di Porta Ticinese, is again an area for younger, trendier fashions, with ethnic shops.

Interior Design

Milan is also the world's leading centre for furniture and household design, and the city is home to a large number of stylish stores and showrooms of leading producers. You can find some of the leading names along Via Durini, familiarly known as 'Design Street', and also along Corso G. Matteotti, both south of the Quadrilatero d'Oro. High Tech, on Piazza XXV Aprile 12, occupying an ex-factory, is a mecca for design aficionados, with the latest styles in household goods and furniture from all over the world. A courtesy bus will take you to Cargo, the new sister store in Via Meucci.

Department Stores

Milan's most central and upmarket department store is La Rinascente on Piazza del Duomo (open daily until 10pm). Situated right beside the Duomo and with good views of it from the seventh-floor café/restaurant, the store has everything from stylish clothes for men and women to cosmetics and household goods. Coin, in Piazza Cinque Giornate, southeast of the centre, is an affordable chain store with a wide range of clothes and excellent-value accessories as well as household goods.

Bags of style in Milan's shop windows

Books, Music and Multimedia

Milan has a wide range of bookshops, from megastores open seven days a week, evenings included, to small specialist shops keeping regular opening hours. In Galleria Vittorio Emanuele II, Rizzoli is a well-stocked, popular bookshop and one of the best for guides on Milan and art books; also in the Galleria, Ricordi Mediastore has a good choice of classical and modern music. This is owned by Feltrinelli, who has bookshops on Piazza Duomo (on the corner with Via U. Foscolo), Via Manzoni and Piazza Cavour, which sell English-language books. IT fans will enjoy the Mondadori Multicenter on Via Marghera 28, west of the centre, a huge store of books, DVDs, gifts, computer software, electronics, and an internet café with 20 connection points.

Shopping Knowledge

Milanese shop assistants can be frosty, particularly if you don't look the part or you handle the merchandise. But, of course, they all like a sale, and if you look like a potential buyer they will be very willing to help. Many stores will arrange to have your shopping bags taken back to your hotel – leaving you hands-free for more retail therapy.

The busiest times, particularly in and around the Quadrilatero d'Oro, are the fashion weeks at the end of February and the beginning of October, and the sales in July and August and January/February, when there are long queues outside the shops for cut-price designer items.

Shops are normally open from Monday afternoon to Saturday evening. Some close from 1pm–3.30pm, though an increasing number of designer stores are staying open over the lunch break. Closing time is usually 7 or 7.30pm, though during the fashion and furniture fairs many shops extend their opening hours. Large bookshops and some of the megastores are also open on Sundays.

Gastronomy

Gourmets will enjoy the city's food shops, stacked with everything from home-cured hams, speciality risotto rice, herbs and honey to local wines, grappa and liqueurs. The legendary Milanese deli is Peck (Via Spadari 9, near the Pinacoteca Ambrosiana), a stunning showcase of the finest cheeses and hams, pasta and pastries, smoked wild salmon and spectacular truffles – all under the same roof, along with a café, wine bar and basement wine cellar. The spit-roasted chickens and hot pasta at the Peck Rotisserie around the corner on Via Cesare Cantù make great take-aways. For delicious cakes and pastries, including a legendary *panettone*, the Milanese Christmas cake, go to Marchesi, on Via Santa Maria alla Porta 13, an old-fashioned *pasticceria*. Wine connoisseurs will enjoy a visit to the Enoteca Cotti at Via Solferino 42, a long-established shop stocking around 1,000 fine wines and hundred of grappas and liqueurs.

Gourmet food shop

Markets and Antiques

Colourful street markets sell everything from flowers and fruit to fashions and household goods. A great choice for clothing and accessories, including designer-label bargains, is the huge (and very crowded) Mercato di Viale Papiniano, Porta Genova, held on Tuesday morning and all day Saturday.

At the Navigli market

The Saturday Fiera di Sinigaglia, now at the Darsena on Viale d'Annunzio, is another good source, with new and vintage clothes and accessories. The colourful and crowded flea market (metro S. Donato) takes place on Sunday mornings. Every third Saturday of the month, except in August, the Brera is the venue of the Mercato dell'Antiquariato (Antique Market), with stalls selling antiques, bric-a-brac and jewellery. But the most extensive and colourful antiques market is held in the Navigli quarter on the last Sunday of the month (except July), with over 400 stalls spreading along the Naviglio Grande. Bargaining at any of the markets is worth a try, however limited your Italian.

ENTERTAINMENT

Milan is home to one of the world's most prestigious opera houses, along with dozens of theatres, cinemas, concert venues and art galleries. It also offers the most vibrant nightlife in Italy, with live rock and pop concerts and scores of stylish bars and nightclubs drawing Italians from all corners of the country.

The tourist office in Piazza del Duomo supplies listings and can sell tickets for most events. Useful free publications to pick up while you are there are *Milano Mese* or the paper

Hello Milano (also available from <www.hellomilano.it>), both packed with city listings and other useful information. The Wednesday edition of the daily *Corriere della Sera* newspaper has listings in the *ViviMilano* supplement, and *La Repubblica* likewise in its Thursday *TuttoMilano* section.

Opera, Theatre and Cinema

For many visitors Milan means opera. The Teatro alla Scala, or La Scala as it is more familiarly known, hosts ballet and classical concerts as well as opera *(see pages 34–5)*. The opera season runs from 7 December and continues through to July. Ballet and classical concerts are held here during the autumn months.

For information on ticket availability visit <www.teatroallascala.org> or telephone the Scala Infotel service on 02 72003744 (9am–6pm daily). Seating plans and the season's programme can be viewed on the website. Tickets can be purchased either via the automatic telephone-booking service on 02 860775 (24-hour service in four languages) up to two weeks before the performance, or online via the Teatro alla Scala website (see above, credit card payment only, with 20 percent surcharge).

The central box office (daily noon–6pm) is in the Duomo metro station opposite the ATM public transport office. One month before the performances take place all unsold tickets are put on sale here. Two hours before

> There are numerous annual events in and around the city, from the famous fashion shows to long-established festivals rooted in historic or religious events. Exhibitions are currently held at both the 'old' trade centre, Fiera Milano City, and the brand new complex, Fiera Milano, just outside Milan in Rho-Pero (<www.fieramilano.it>).

Performance at a packed-out La Scala

the performance, 140 numbered tickets for gallery seats are sold at the Evening Box Office, which is near the opera house. Any last-minute tickets that are still available in the hour before the performance are usually sold at around a 25 percent discount.

If your Italian is up to it, there are dozens of theatres that cater for all tastes, offering a wide choice of entertainment, from traditional to avant-garde drama, musicals, dance and cabaret. The most prestigious are the Piccolo Teatro Strehler (Largo Greppi), named after the renowned director Giorgio Strehler, and the Teatro Grassi (Via Rovello 2), which also has performances in English. (Information for both theatres at <www.piccoloteatro.org>.)

For other theatre information consult the Milan section of <www.teatrionline.com>. Multiplex cinemas are concentrated in the city centre. Foreign-language films are normally dubbed into Italian.

Concerts

Milan offers a whole gamut of music, from classical concerts and choral music performances to live jazz and rock. The Conservatorio di Musica Giuseppe Verdi at Via Conservatorio 12 (<www.consmilano.it>) hosts regular classical concerts in a former monastery from mid-September to June; the 1,400-seat Auditorium di Milano (<www.auditoriumdimilano.org>) in the Ticinese quarter is home to the Symphonic Orchestra of Giuseppe Verdi and hosts symphony concerts, choral and chamber music and jazz and light music.

Classical concerts are held in churches throughout the city, among them San Marco, San Simpliciano, Santa Maria del Carmine and San Maurizio. Open-air concerts are held in summer at the Castello Sforzesco and other venues around the city.

Tickets for concerts can be bought at stores throughout the city, including Ricordi in the Galleria Vittorio Emanuele II and FNAC on Via Torino (on the corner with Via della Palla), both of which are in the centre.

Bars, Nightclubs and Discos

The Brera and in particular the Navigli canal district are packed out with bars and clubs where you can relax with a drink, listen to jazz or rock, or dance until the early hours of the morning. Other hotspots are Porta Romana, Corso Sempione, Corso Como and the up-and-coming Isola district just north of Stazione Garibaldi.

The best time to spot the film stars, footballers and fashion models is in the early evening, when they can be seen sipping cocktails at hip bars and cafés. The pre-prandial *aperitivo*, from around 6–8 or 9pm, has become part of the Milanese way of life. The price of the drink may seem steep, but snacks, canapés and sometimes a whole buffet (say couscous, sushi, curry or cheese) is included and can provide a cheap alternative to dinner in a restaurant. Many venues are cafés during the day and turn into nightclubs or discos from 11pm.

Ultra-chic venues, frequented by the fashion crowd, are the bar and garden of the Bulgari Hotel (Via Fratelli Gabba 7b; <www.bugarihotels.com>), the Straf Bar of the Straf Hotel (Via S. Raffaele 3; <www.straf.it>), Corso Como 10 and Robert Cavalli's Just Cavalli Café, at the foot of the Torre Branca in Parco Sempione (<www.justcavallicafe.com>). Expect a range of décor, from minimalist Japanese style to lavish interiors, palm trees and African prints. The Absolut Icebar (Townhouse 12 Hotel, Piazza Gerusalemme 12; <www.townhouse.it/icebar>) is literally the coolest spot – at minus 5 degrees! Walls, floor and bar are all made of ice, and the only drink is vodka and fruit juice. Cloaks and boots are provided, but you are not likely to last long. (Entrance fee of €15 includes one drink and 25 minutes' exposure.)

Alcatraz (Via Valtellina 25; <www.alcatrazmilano.com>) is the city's biggest disco, occupying a former factory and hosting occasional live shows, rock concerts and cabarets; Hollywood (Corso Como 15; <www.discotecahollywood.com>) lives up to its name, being famous for celebrities (entry at the doorman's discretion). Rolling Stone (Corso XXII Marzo 42; <www.rollingstone.it>) is hugely popular for rock music and concerts, and Blue Note (Via Borsieri 37; <www.bluenotemilano.com>) is the best for live jazz.

Pop concerts take place at Filaforum (<www.forumnet.it>), at Assago just out of Milan, with a capacity for 12,000, or at Palavobis Music Village, Via Sant'Elia 33 (tel: 02 542754).

> **All public venues in Italy are non-smoking unless they have a separate section for smokers. Most places cannot afford a non-smoking section, hence the abundance of cigarette stubs on the pavements outside bars and restaurants.**

SPORT

Football is the main sport associated with Milan, and after Italy's victory in the 2006 World Cup, it is more popular than ever. The city has two of the world's top football teams: Inter and AC Milan, both of which play at the Giuseppe Meazza San Siro Stadium, west of the city centre at Via Piccolomini 5 (metro MM1 Lotto, then tram 16). The teams play on alternate Sundays from September to May; for tickets visit <www.acmilan.com> and <www.inter.it>.

Jogger in the Giardini Pubblici

Another great spectator venue is the Formula One circuit at Monza, which hosts the Italian Grand Prix in early September. Monza lies northeast of Milan, and can be reached in 15 minutes by train from Stazione Centrale or Garibaldi.

For a break from the heat and traffic, you could head east to Milan's Idropark Fila, otherwise known as 'Milan's Sea'. Built in 1928 as a landing for seaplanes, it is a huge artificial lake with a water park, rowing regattas, canoeing and boating. The park and surroundings provide jogging trails and opportunities for free climbing and mountain biking. Close to Linate Airport, the park is at Viale dell'Idroscalo 1 (tel: 02 7560393; bus No. 73 from Milan's Piazza San Babila).

If you don't mind crowds, you could go along to the Lido di Milano south of the city centre (Piazzale Lotto 15; tel: 02

392791; metro MM1 Lotto), which has tennis courts, outdoor swimming pool with slides, gym, windsurfing and minigolf.

There are several golf courses in the Milan area, the best of which is the Milano Golf Club, which is out at Monza (<www.golfclubmilano.it>).

CHILDREN

Milan holds little fascination for young visitors, and unless they are immaculately behaved (and dressed) they won't be given a warm welcome in the fashion salons. As for sightseeing, youngsters might enjoy clambering on the roof of the Duomo *(see page 27)*, going to the top of the Torre Branca *(see page 46)*, or visiting the Natural History Museum at Corso Venezia 55 *(see page 56)*. The Science Museum *(see page 62)* exhibits huge boats, steam trains and aircraft, and there are interactive labs where you can make industrial soap bubbles or touch a bolt of lightning. Football enthusiasts will enjoy a match at Milan's San Siro Stadium *(see page 93)* or a visit to the stadium museum (Gate 21, Via Piccolomini 5; open daily 10am–5pm, but variable on match days). The museum has life-size statues of AC Milan and Inter heroes, and includes a visit to the stadium.

On top of the Duomo

The Museo dei Bambini (Via Matteo Bandello 18; <www.muba.it>; admission fee) puts on interactive children's exhibitions designed to stimulate creativity. The Museo del Giocattolo e del Bambino (Via Pitteri 56; <www.museodelgiocattolo.it>) is one of Europe's largest toy museums, with 2,000 exhibits, dating from 1700.

Calendar of Events

6 January (Epiphany) *Corteo dei Magi* – historical procession of the Three Kings from the Duomo to Sant'Eustorgio.
February Carnival celebrating Sant'Ambrogio, continuing all the way through to the first Saturday of Lent. Parades with floats around the Duomo and centre, religious services and special events for children. *Milano Moda Donna* – Italian fashion designers present their autumn and winter collections in Milan; trade only, by invitation, but there are concerts and other events in the city, organised around the fashion shows (mid-Feb). BIT (Borsa Internazionale del Turismo) – Italy's most important tourist trade show (mid-Feb).
End March/early April Milan International Film Festival.
April *Salone Internazionale del Mobile* – the largest furniture exhibition in Europe, with the latest Italian and foreign designs on display.
May *Orticola* – an increasingly popular three-day fair in early May devoted to flowers and plants, held in the Giardini Pubblici. *Pittori sul Naviglio* – two-day exhibition, when over 200 artists from all over Italy exhibit works along the banks of the Naviglio Grande.
First Sunday of June Milan's *Festa dei Navigli* – antiques and craft stalls, boat races, street performers and concerts in the Navigli canal district.
July and August *Festival Latino-Americano* – two months of Latin American concerts and shows held at the Assago Forum.
September *Italian Grand Prix* – Formula One racing at Monza (first week). *Milano Moda Donna* – Spring and summer fashion collections at Fiera-Milano (<www.fieramilano.com>, <www.cameramoda.com>); trade only, by invitation (end of September).
Mid-October SMAU – major international information and communications technology trade show (<www.smau.it>).
7 December Grand opening of Milan's La Scala opera season. This is also the Festa di Sant'Ambrogio, Milan's favourite feast day, celebrating the city's patron saint. During the *Fiera degli O Bej O Bej*, held on 7 and 8 December, market stalls are set up in the streets around the Basilica di Sant'Ambrogio, selling antiques, crafts, flowers and food.

EATING OUT

Milan's culinary scene caters for all tastes, from local rustic fare, through pizzas and fast food, to sushi and 'fusion'. The influx of immigrant workers from other parts of Italy in the 1950s gave rise to a variety of Italian regional cuisine, particularly Tuscan and southern Italian. A second wave of immigrants in the 1980s and 1990s, this time from further afield, ensured a wide ethnic variety. Today you can find Japanese, Chinese, Thai, Indian, Middle Eastern, North African and American – just to name a few.

Though sushi may be the rage, classic Milanese fare manages to survive. It is highly varied, sourcing ingredients from nearby lakes, mountains and flatlands, and, unlike most other regions of Italy, the locals prefer their food rich and creamy. Rice, rather than pasta, is the mainstay of their diet, grown on the vast paddy fields of the Po Valley. Lombardy also produces large amounts of corn, which is made into polenta (cornmeal), served with many of the Milanese main courses.

Meat and dairy produce are abundant, and butter, rather than olive oil, is used in Lombard cuisine. Risotto here is simmered in butter with onion, then cooked slowly with stock added bit by bit. Local cheeses, ranging from the parmesan-like Grana Padana to the creamy cow's-milk cheeses, appear

> The work ethic of Milan precludes the typical Italian two-to-three-hour lunch break, and though there are still plenty of restaurants where you can linger over four courses, the city is also packed with sandwich bars and fast-food outlets, especially around the Duomo. A sign of the times is the success of Brek, an Italian self-service chain *(see page 139)*.

Alfresco dining in the lively Brera neighbourhood

on every menu, either enriching pastas and risottos or served on a platter with fresh bread and olive oil. Fresh herbs and vegetables, such as *porcini* mushrooms, artichokes, red chicory and asparagus, are key ingredients, grown in abundance and used with fish, meat, risotto and pasta. Milan has the biggest fish market in Italy, ensuring a wide variety of both freshwater fish and seafood to choose from in restaurants throughout the city.

WHERE TO EAT

Although traditionally a **ristorante** is smarter, more professional and expensive than a **trattoria**, the difference between the two these days is negligible. An **osteria**, traditionally a tavern or inn serving wine and pasta, can nowadays be any type of restaurant, from traditional to hip.

The ubiquitous **pizzeria** usually offers a wide-ranging menu including many pasta and meat dishes, and even fish,

Buon appetito!

as well as pizzas. But do not assume pizzeria means a cheap meal. Many have brought their prices into line with trattorias and restaurants. The best of the pizzas come bubbling hot from a wood-fired brick oven, while the worst are thick-based squares with a thin layer of tomato and cheese topping, served in cafés during the day. *Pizza a taglio*, sold by the slice with a variety of toppings, is the most popular Italian take-away.

An **enoteca** or wine bar will have a wide selection of fine wines with a platter of cheese or cold meats to accompany them. A **tavola calda** is a self-service or take-away with hot dishes such as pasta, risottos, meat and vegetable dishes. A **rosticceria** serves roast chicken, pasta and other hot dishes to eat in or take away.

For a quick bite, go to a **bar** or **café**, where you can find a selection of rolls with savoury fillings and *tramezzini* (crustless, generously filled sandwiches). Standing at the bar, as the locals tend to do, is always a lot cheaper than sitting at a table with waiter service.

Most restaurants open for lunch from 12.30–3pm and dinner from 7 to around 10pm. Pizzerias and ethnic restaurants often stay open much later, until around midnight. Many restaurants close for August – or at least part of it.

WHAT TO EAT

As in the rest of Italy, restaurants (as opposed to pizzerias) offer four courses: the *antipasto* (hors d'oeuvre), *primo* (the first course, which is usually pasta, risotto or soup), *secondo* (the second main course, i.e. fish or meat) and the *dolce* (dessert) – followed perhaps by cheese, coffee and a *digestivo*. Traditionally, you were expected to have at least three courses; nowadays, in most establishments it's quite acceptable to opt, say, for an *antipasto* followed by a pasta, or perhaps a pasta followed by a dessert.

Antipasti

The selection of hors d'oeuvre will typically include an *antipasto di carne* or *affettati misti,* a selection of cold meats such as thinly sliced *prosciutto crudo* (Parma ham), mountain hams, *salame di cinghiale* (wild-boar salami), seasoned sausages and *Bresaola* (air-dried beef), served with lemon, olive oil and black pepper. *Insalata di mare* (seafood salad) will be a plate of seafood such as prawns, mussels, squid and octopus; *antipasto di pesce* (fish) may be a selection of marinated seafood or lake fish such as *persico* (perch), *tinca* (tench) or *lavarello* (a white fish). Vegetable *antipasti* are likely to feature *peperoni* (sweet peppers), *zucchini* (courgettes), *melanzane* (aubergine or eggplant) and *carciofi* (artichokes).

Primi

Rice is prepared in dozens of different ways, enriched with fish, seafood, meat or vegetables. The ingredients will vary according to the season. The most famous local rice dish is *risotto alla milanese,* made with Arborio or Carnaroli rice, slowly cooked with onions, beef marrow and stock, served with liberal amounts of butter and Parmesan cheese and – what makes it distinctly Milanese – flavoured and coloured with saffron. Other popular combinations are *risotto ai funghi*, cooked with mushrooms (particularly delicious are the *porcini* or wild mushrooms in the autumn) and *risotto alla pescatora* with prawns, squid, mussels and clams.

Pasta comes in all shapes and sizes, is often home-made and, like risotto, is served with a remarkable range of sauces. Along with the local specialities you can always find the long-standing favourites such as *al pomodoro*, tomato sauce flavoured with onion, garlic or basil, *alla carbonara*, with eggs, bacon, parmesan and pecorino cheeses, *al ragù*, the Neapolitan meat sauce, or *alle vongole*, with clams.

Soups can be a meal in themselves, especially the delicious *zuppa di pesce*, more of a fish stew than a soup and made with several types of fish. *Minestrone alla milanese,* a vegetable soup with rice and bacon, is widely available; other soups include *zuppa pavese*, a clear broth with egg and bread, and *zuppa di cipolle*, onion soup.

Stuffed courgette flowers with salad garnish

Secondi

The classic Milanese meat dish is *osso buco*, veal shank from milk-fed calves, slowly braised with wine, topped with *gremolada* (also spelt *gremolata*) – a paste of chopped garlic, lemon zest and parsley – and served with *risotto alla milanese*. Other local dishes include *cotoletta alla Milanese*, veal cutlet dipped in egg, coated in breadcrumbs and lightly fried in butter (which across the border in Austria goes by the name of *Wiener schnitzel*) and *cassoeula*, a wintry dish of pork cuts, sausage and savoy cabbage, cooked for several hours and usually served with polenta.

Today's menu

Beef, veal, ox tongue and spiced pork sausage are typical ingredients of *bollito misto* or boiled meats, often served with *mostarda di Cremona*, a sauce of mustard-flavoured preserved fruits. This meat dish is something of an acquired taste, as is the local *fritto misto*, a fry-up of veal liver, brains, lungs, sweetbreads and meat croquettes, usually served with mushrooms, artichokes or courgettes. You may also come across braised donkey, jugged hare and stewed tripe, risotto with frogs' legs, and boiled snails prepared with fennel, anchovies and white wine.

For more conventional tastes, there is no problem finding simply cooked steak, pork, veal, lamb and poultry (especially duck, turkey and goose). The choice will vary according to the season. Any meat (or fish) '*alla milanese*' is likely to be coated in breadcrumbs and fried.

Milan may be landlocked, but a huge variety of fresh fish is delivered daily. As well as specialist fish and seafood restaurants, there are dozens of places offering just as much fish as meat. Freshwater fish is sourced from the River Po or Alpine lakes, and seafood from Italian shores and beyond. Commonly found on menus are *branzino* (bass), *orata* (bream), *sogliola* (sole), *gamberoni* (giant prawns), *calamari* (squid) and *vongole* (clams). Salted and dried cod (*bacalà*) is used in dozens of recipes. Many restaurants use frozen fish, and some of the more upfront ones will indicate this with a star against the item. Smaller fish are served whole at a fixed price, but the larger species will be charged by the *etto* (100g), and it's wise to check the price before ordering.

Main courses often come with *contorni* (vegetables); salads are ordered and served separately and are almost invariably *verde* (green) or *mista* (mixed). Vegetarian restaurants have been springing up in recent years, and many restaurants now offer at least one meat- and fish-free dish. You might try grilled vegetables as an *antipasto*, then a risotto or pasta with fresh *porcini* or other vegetables; or maybe splash out on the 13-course tasting menu at Joia *(see page 139)*, one of the best vegetarian restaurants in Italy.

Milanese Brunch

Brunch has become a weekend way of life for the Milanese. On Saturdays and Sundays, from around 10am until 2–4pm, clubs and cafés offer a lavish American/Italian-style buffet of brioches, croissants, muffins, eggs, bacon, pastas, risottos, cold meats and cheeses. Favourite and fashionable venues, where you are likely to spot celebrities, are the garden of the Hotel Sheraton Diana Majestic, Viale Piave 42; Old Fashion Café, Palazzo dell'Arte, Viale Alemagna 6, in Parco Sempione; and Tribeca Lounge, Via Conca del Naviglio 22.

Dolci

Depending on the restaurant, for a *dolce* you may be offered anything from a fruit salad or *gelato* (ice cream) to a whole trolley of elaborate home-made desserts and cakes. *Panettone*, the domed cake containing eggs, butter, raisins and candied fruit, was originally a Milanese dessert, but is now a famous Christmas cake found all over the country, and increasingly abroad. Many restaurants serve *tiramisù* (literally 'pick-me-up'), the alcoholic chocolate and coffee gateau from the Veneto. As an alternative, you could do as many Milanese do and buy a

Freshly baked tarts

gelato from a local *gelateria*. Some have up to 100 varieties.

Cheese platters are laden with delicious Lombard varieties, from the creamy, blue-veined Gorgonzola, the soft and pungent Taleggio, the fresh, creamy Stracchino and Robiolo, to the tangy Provolone Valpadano and the hard Grana cheese produced in the Po Valley.

Wines and Liqueurs

Lombardy is not one of the famous wine-producing regions of Italy, and, in terms of quantity, its output can't match that of neighbouring Piedmont, Emilia-Romagna and the Veneto. It does, however, produce some excellent wines, the most notable being the dry, smooth reds from Valtellina on the

Enjoying a leisurely family meal in the Navigli quarter

Italian/Swiss border. The region's most productive zone is Oltrepò Pavese, in the Po Valley south of Pavia, noted for some good Pinots and robust Barbera, Bonarda and Oltrepò Pavese Rosso; it also produces Pinot sparkling wine and a large quantity of fruity white Riesling. The hilly Franciacorta region near Brescia produces sturdy reds as well as white wines, but is best-known for its Champagne-style sparkling *Spumante*, which makes an excellent aperitif.

Restaurants invariably offer wines from other regions, such as the Barolos from Piedmont or Chiantis from Tuscany, and the more expensive restaurants will offer international as well as Italian wines. House wine, *vino della casa*, is usually acceptable and always reasonably priced. In the cheaper places it's served in litre or half-litre carafes or jugs.

A good meal is frequently concluded with a *digestivo*, such as a brandy, grappa (the variable local firewater made from grape skins) or *limoncello*, from lemons.

To Help you Order…

A table for one/two/three please	**Un tavolo per una persona/per due/per tre**
I would like…	**Vorrei…**
The bill please	**Il conto per favore**
What would you recommend?	**Cosa ci consiglia?**

…and Read the Menu

aglio	garlic	**maiale**	pork
agnello	lamb	**manzo**	beef
aragosta	lobster	**melanzane**	aubergine
basilico	basil	**olio**	oil
birra	beer	**olive**	olives
bistecca	beefsteak	**panna**	cream
burro	butter	**pane**	bread
calamari	squid	**patate**	potatoes
carciofi	artichokes	**peperoni**	peppers
cavallo	horse	**pesce**	fish
cinghiale	wild boar	**piselli**	peas
cipolle	onions	**pollo**	chicken
coniglio	rabbit	**polpo/pólipo**	octopus
cozze	mussels	**pomodori**	tomatoes
fagioli	beans	**prosciutto**	ham
fagiolini	green beans	**riso**	rice
finocchio	fennel	**salsiccie**	sausages
formaggio	cheese	**spinaci**	spinach
frittata	omelette	**tonno**	tuna
frutti di mare	seafood	**uova**	eggs
funghi	mushrooms	**verdure**	vegetables
gamberetti	shrimps	**vitello**	veal
gamberi	prawns	**vino**	wine
gelato	ice cream	**vongole**	clams
insalata	salad	**zucchini**	courgettes
lumache	snails	**zuppa**	soup

HANDY TRAVEL TIPS

An A–Z Summary of Practical Information

- **A** Accommodation 107
  - Airports 108
- **B** Budgeting for Your Trip 109
- **C** Camping 109
  - Car Hire 109
  - Climate 110
  - Crime and Safety 110
  - Customs and Entry Requirements 110
- **D** Disabled Travellers 111
  - Driving 111
- **E** Electricity 113
  - Embassies and Consulates 113
  - Emergencies 113
- **G** Gay and Lesbian Travellers 114
  - Getting There 114
  - Guides and Tours 115
- **H** Health and Medical Care 115
- **L** Language 116
- **M** Media 117
  - Money 117
- **O** Opening Hours 118
- **P** Police 119
  - Post Offices 119
  - Public Holidays 120
  - Public Transport 120
- **R** Religion 122
- **S** Smoking 122
- **T** Telephones 123
  - Time Differences 124
  - Tipping 124
  - Toilets 125
  - Tourist Information 125
- **W** Websites and Internet 126
  - Weights and Measures 127
- **Y** Youth Hostels 127

A

ACCOMMODATION (See also Camping, Youth Hostels, and the list of Recommended Hotels on page 128)

All hotels are officially categorised from one to five stars, or, at the very top, five-star de luxe. The stars assigned denote amenities, and are no indicator of charm or atmosphere. Prices depend on season, location and category. During trade fairs, and especially fashion and design shows, prices rocket, and rooms are reserved months in advance. Some of the best deals are in August, when many Milanese head for the coast, or at weekends, when business hotels are empty.

If you make a reservation by phone, hotels require confirmation by email or fax. A deposit of one night's stay, payable by credit card, is usually requested. Failure to turn up or to inform the hotel in advance of cancellation will normally incur the loss of the deposit. Room rates include local taxes and service charges, but beware of VAT (IVA) charges (20 percent on five-star hotels and 10 percent on other categories), which are sometimes added to the bill. Breakfast, which can be anything from a dull crusty roll to a great spread of cheese, cold meats, cereals, croissants and fruit, is normally included in the overnight room rate. If not, it is usually better value to grab a cappuccino and croissant from a local café than pay for the hotel breakfast.

If you arrive on spec, the IAT office on Piazza del Duomo *(see page 126)* can supply hotel information but will not make the bookings for you. However, the tourist offices at the Stazione Centrale and at Linate and Malpensa airports provide booking facilities. For information on hotels and online booking visit <www.initalia.it>.

I'd like a single/ double room	**Vorrei una camera singola/ matrimoniale**
with bath/shower	**con bagno/doccia.**
What's the rate per night?	**Quanto si paga per notte?**

AIRPORTS

Milan has three main airports. Easily the most convenient for the centre is **Linate** (tel: 02 74852200, <www.sea-aeroportimilano.it>), 10km (6 miles) east of Milan, which handles mainly domestic and European flights. The Starfly shuttle (<www.autostradale.com>) operates a half-hourly service to Milan's Stazione Centrale, taking 25 minutes, and the No. 73 bus (<www.atm-mi.it>) departs every 10 minutes to Piazza San Babila in the city centre. During trade fairs there is also an hourly bus service from Linate to the trade centre.

Malpensa airport (tel: 02 26800613/74852200; <www.sea-aeroportimilano.it>), 50km (31 miles) northwest of the city, services national, international and intercontinental flights. The airport is linked to Milan's Cadorna station by the half-hourly Malpensa Express train (<www.ferrovienord.it>). Trains run every half-hour and take 45 minutes. The Malpensa Shuttle (<www.malpensashuttle.it>) and the Malpensa Bus Express (<www.autostradale.com>) provide regular coach services to Stazione Centrale, taking 50–60 minutes.

Orio al Serio airport (tel: 035 326323, <www.sacbo.it>) is at Bergamo, 48km (30 miles) northeast of Milan, and is used by Ryanair and other low-cost airlines. A half-hourly shuttle bus service goes to Stazione Centrale, taking just over an hour, and is operated by two different companies: Autostradale (tel: 035 318472, <www.autostradale.com>) and the cheaper Locatelli Air Pullman (<www.orioshuttle.com>). Both services take 65 minutes. All three airports are equipped with banks, currency exchange, cash machines, tourist office, hotel booking facilities, left luggage and internet access.

Could you please take these bags to the bus/train/taxi?	**Mi porti queste valige fino all' autobus/al treno/al taxi per favore?**
What time does the train/bus leave for the city centre?	**A che ora parte il treno/ pullman per il centro?**

B

BUDGETING FOR YOUR TRIP

Milan is one of the most expensive cities in Italy. You can expect to pay €120–250 for a comfortable double room with bath, €90–120 for a double in a simple hotel or B&B. A good three-course meal in a restaurant without wine costs from €30–50 upwards, a sandwich with a drink and coffee €8–12, coffee or soft drinks €1.50–2.50, cocktail with nibbles or buffet included €6–10. As in the rest of Italy, coffee or drinks taken at the bar are considerably cheaper than those served at a table. A ticket for the metro, bus or tram is €1. Use of a public internet point is around €3 an hour. Entry fees to museums, archaeological sites and gardens vary from €2–8; entrance is free for EU citizens under 18 and over 65.

C

CAMPING

The nearest campsite to Milan is the Camping Città di Milano at Via Gaetano Airaghi 61 (tel: 02 48207017, <www.campingmilano.it>), 8km (5 miles) west of the city. This is a well-equipped, four-star site next to the Aquatica water park, with its own swimming pool, sports facilities and restaurant. It is open all year except December and January. Details of campsites in the Lombardy region are available on the internet at <www.camping.it>. The Touring Club Italiano also has useful information on camping at <www.touring club.it>, but full details are only accessible on payment of the €25 membership fee.

CAR HIRE (See also DRIVING)

The major rental companies have outlets at Milan's airports and at the Stazione Centrale. A small car will cost from around €250 a week, including third-party liability and taxes, but excluding insurance excess. Drivers must present their own national driving licence or one that is internationally recognised.

CLIMATE

The best time to go to Milan is spring, early summer or autumn. July and August are uncomfortably hot, with temperatures of around 30°C (86°F), and in August many businesses, restaurants and shops close down. Winter months tend to be foggy and cold, and snow is not uncommon.

The chart below shows the maximum average temperature in Milan, per month.

	J	F	M	A	M	J	J	A	S	O	N	D
°C	5	8	13	18	23	27	29	29	24	17	10	6
°F	40	46	56	65	74	80	84	85	75	63	51	43

CRIME AND SAFETY

It is wise to take precautions against pickpockets. Leave important documents and valuables in the hotel safe, and keep a firm hold of handbags, especially in crowded locations. For insurance purposes, theft and loss must be reported immediately to the police. Beware of vendors selling fake merchandise in the city centre, particularly silk.

| I want to report a theft. | **Vorrei denunciare un furto.** |
| My wallet/passport/ticket has been stolen. | **Mi hanno rubato il portafoglio/il passaporto/il biglietto.** |

CUSTOMS AND ENTRY REQUIREMENTS

For citizens of EU countries a valid passport or identity card is all that is needed to enter Italy for stays of up to 90 days. Citizens of US, Canada, Australia and New Zealand require only a valid passport.

Visas *(permesso di soggiorno)*. For stays of more than 90 days a visa or residence permit is required. Contact the Italian embassy in your country.

Customs. Free exchange of non-duty-free goods for personal use is allowed between EU countries. Those from non-EU countries should refer to their home country's regulating organisation for a current complete list of import restrictions.

Currency restrictions. Tourists may bring an unlimited amount of Italian or foreign currency into the country. On departure you must declare any currency beyond the equivalent of €12,500, so it's wise to declare sums exceeding this amount when you arrive.

D

DISABLED TRAVELLERS

For information on accessibility within the city, including suggested itineraries, visit <www.milanopertutti.it>, the website of AIAS Milano Onlus (l'Associazione Italiana Assistenza Spastici), Via P. Mantegazza 10 (tel: 02 3302021). Milan's public transport company, ATM, operates an information service specifically for the disabled, the Ufficio Disabili at Foro Bonaparte 61 (tel: 02 4803144; open Mon–Fri 8.30am–12.30pm, 2–4.30pm).

DRIVING

Milan is served by an extensive motorway network connecting the city with the rest of the country, but driving within the city, with its chaotic traffic and one-way streets, is best avoided.

Rules of the road. Drive on the right, overtake on the left. Unless otherwise indicated, speed limits in Italy are 50km/h (30mph) in towns and built-up areas, 90km/h (55mph) on main roads and 130km/h (80mph) on motorways *(autostrade)*. Headlights must be kept on when driving on motorways and state roads *(strade statali)* during the day. At roundabouts the traffic from the right has the right of way. Seat belts are compulsory in the front and back, and children should be properly restrained. The use of hand-held mobile telephones while driving is prohibited. The blood alcohol limit is 0.08 percent, and police occasionally make random breath tests.

Breakdowns. In case of accident or breakdown call 113 (General Emergencies) or the Automobile Club of Italy on 116. The club has an efficient 24-hour service which also has an English-speaking service (tel: 803116).

I've had a breakdown.	**Ho avuto un guasto.**
There's been an accident.	**C'è stato un incidente.**
Fill it up please.	**Faccia il pieno per favore**
super/normal	**super/normale**
lead-free/diesel	**senza piombo/gasolio**
Where's the nearest car park?	**Dov'è il parcheggio più vicino?**
Can I park here?	**Posso parcheggiare qui?**
Are we on the right road for...?	**Siamo sulla strada giusta per...?**

Petrol. Some service stations close over the lunch period and on Saturday afternoons and Sundays, but there are plenty of 24-hour stations with self-service dispensers accepting euro notes and major credit cards.

Parking. Finding a parking space in Milan is notoriously difficult. In the centre, parking is allowed within the blue lines and controlled by SostaMilano 'scratch cards'. These are available from parking attendants, tobacconists, bars, ATM (Azienda Trasporti Milanesi) sales points and news-stands, and must be displayed on the dashboard. Costs are reasonable (around €2 for two hours). For privately run car parks visit <www.parcheggiomilano.it>. Various reasonably priced park-and-ride schemes enable you to leave your car outside the centre and travel in by bus or metro. For information visit <www.atm-mi.it> (some of the details are in Italian only).

E

ELECTRICITY

220V/50Hz AC is standard. Sockets take two-pin, round-pronged plugs. UK appliances will require an adaptor, American 110V appliances a transformer.

EMBASSIES AND CONSULATES

If you lose your passport or need other help, contact your nearest national embassy or consulate.
Australia: Australian Consulate General, Via Borgogna 2, tel: 02 77704227), <www.italy.embassy.gov.au>
Canada: Canadian Consulate General, Via Vittor Pisani 19, tel: 02 67581, <www.canada.it>
Ireland: Piazza S. Pietro in Gessate 2, tel: 02 55187569
New Zealand: Via Guido D'Arezzo 6, tel: 02 4990201, email: <nzemb.rom@flashnet.it>
UK: Via San Paolo 7, tel: 02 723001, <www.britain.it>
US: Via Principe Amedeo 2/10, tel: 02 290351, <www.usembassy.it>

EMERGENCIES

Police   112
General Emergency   113
Fire   115
Ambulance   118

Local doctors are on call for emergencies from Monday to Friday and on Sunday from 8pm–8am and on Saturday from 2–8pm, tel: 02 34567.

G

GAY AND LESBIAN TRAVELLERS

Milan is young and cosmopolitan, and arguably offers the best gay scene in Italy. One of the most popular clubs is Nuovo Idea International on Via de Castilla 30, which claims to be the first gay club in Italy.

Arcigay Milano (Via Bezzecca 3, tel: 02 54122225, <www.arcigaymilano.org>, Italian only), the local branch of the Italian gay organisation, is the main point of contact. The 20th anniversary of the Gay and Lesbian Film Festival was celebrated in 2006. It usually takes place each year in June (<www.cinemagaylesbico.com>).

GETTING THERE

By Air. British Airways (tel: 0780 850 9850, <www.ba.com>) and Alitalia (tel: 0870 544 8259, <www.alitalia.com>) operate frequent flights from Heathrow to both Linate and Malpensa airports. BA also flies to Malpensa from Birmingham and Manchester. A regular service from Stansted to Orio al Serio airport at Bergamo is operated by Ryanair (tel: 0871 246 0000, <www.ryanair.com>). EasyJet (tel: 0905 821 0905, <www.easyjet.com>) flies from Gatwick to Linate and Malpensa.

Flying time from London is around two hours.

From the US there are direct flights from main cities, including New York, Boston and Los Angeles. Alitalia (<www.alitalia.com>) and Delta Airlines (<www.delta.com>) offer the widest selection of direct flights.

By Car. The quickest route to Milan from the UK channel ports takes a minimum of 12 hours, over a distance of 1,040km (650 miles). For route-planning, visit the ViaMichelin website at <www.viamichelin.com>, which gives details of the cost of petrol, road tolls (levied on French and Italian motorways) and the Swiss motorway road tax. To bring your car into Italy, you will need an international driving licence or valid national one, car registration documents, red warning triangle in case of breakdown and a national identity sticker for your car. A green insurance card (an extension to your ordinary insurance) is not compulsory but advisable in case of an accident,

By Rail. The quickest route by rail from the UK is by Eurostar (tel: 08705 186186, <www.eurostar.com>) to the Gare du Nord in Paris, changing to the Gare du Lyon for trains to Milan. For information in the UK on tickets, rail passes and to book online, contact Rail Choice (tel: 020 8659 7300, <www.railchoice.co.uk>) and for rail travel within Italy visit <www.trenitalia.com> (tel: 892021).

GUIDES AND TOURS

From Tuesday to Sunday at 9.30am, three-hour city tours depart from Piazza del Duomo. Tickets are available from major hotels and Autostradale (tel: 02 33910794, <www.autostradale.com>), which is located within the tourist office (see TOURIST INFORMATION). From April to July and September and October there are also afternoon tours, departing at 3pm. Open-topped buses, with commentary in eight languages, depart from Piazza Castello every 45 minutes, less frequently off season (tel: 02 867131, <www.milano.city-sightseeing.it>). For dining on a tram while it circles the city see ATMosfera under Restaurants *(see page 137)*.

H

HEALTH AND MEDICAL CARE

All EU countries have reciprocal arrangements for reclaiming the costs of medical services. UK residents should obtain the EHIC (European Health Insurance Card), available from post offices or online at <www.ehic.org.uk>. This only covers you for medical care, not for emergency repatriation costs or additional expenses such as accommodation and flights for anyone travelling with you. To cover all eventualities a travel insurance policy is advisable, and for non-EU residents essential. For insurance claims keep all receipts for medical treatment and any medicines prescribed.

Vaccinations are not needed for Italy, but take with you sunscreen and mosquito repellent in the summer. Tap water is safe to drink unless you see the sign *Acqua non potabile*. However, many visitors prefer to do as the locals and drink mineral water.

Pharmacies. A pharmacy *(farmacia)* is identified by a green cross. After-hours locations are posted on all pharmacy doors. An all-night service is available at the Stazione Centrale (Central Station) on the first-floor gallery (tel: 02 6690935). Italian pharmacists are well trained to deal with minor ailments and, although they do not stock quantities of foreign medicines, they can usually supply the local equivalent. If you need a doctor *(medico)*, ask at the pharmacy or your hotel. For serious cases or emergencies, dial 118 for an ambulance or head for the *Pronto Soccorso* (Accident and Emergency) of the local hospital. This will also deal with emergency dental treatment.

I need a doctor/dentist.	**Ho bisogno di un medico/dentista.**
Where is the nearest chemist?	**Dov'è la farmacia più vicina?**

L

LANGUAGE

Staff in the main hotels and shops normally speak English. In the more out of the way places a smattering of Italian will come in useful, and any attempt will be appreciated.

MEDIA

Newspapers. The main English and foreign newspapers are available on the day of publication from news-stands in the centre. Listings for the city can be found in the Wednesday edition of the Milan-based *Corriere della Sera* in the *ViviMilano* section and in the *TuttoMilano* section of the Thursday edition of *La Repubblica*.

Television and Radio. Most Milan hotels provide satellite TV, broadcasting 24-hour English-speaking news channels. The Italian state TV network, RAI (Radio Televisione Italiana) broadcasts three TV channels, RAI 1, 2 and 3, and there are half a dozen private channels pouring out soaps, films, quiz shows and non-stop advertisements. The state-run radio stations, RAI 1, 2 and 3, mainly broadcast news, chat and music.

MONEY

Currency. Since January 2002 the unit of currency in Italy has been the euro (€), divided into 100 cents. Euro notes come in denominations of 500, 200, 100, 50, 20, 10 and 5; coins come in denominations of 2 and 1, then 50, 20, 10, 5, 2 and 1 cents.

Exchange facilities. Banks and post offices tend to offer the best rates, followed by exchange offices *(cambio)* and hotels. Some exchange offices offer commission-free facilities, but check first that the rate of exchange is not higher than that of the banks. *Cambio* are usually open daily 8.30am–7.30pm; some may close on Sunday. Travellers' cheques can be exchanged on presentation of a passport at banks and most exchange offices, but not at post offices. The cheques provide security in that they can only be used by the purchaser, and if lost or stolen they will be refunded; however, they attract a high commission, and sometimes a transaction fee on top.

Credit cards and cash machines. The major international credit cards are accepted in the majority of hotels, restaurants, stores and supermarkets. ATM cash machines *(Bancomats)* are widespread, but banks take a hefty commission – it is usually better value to use cash only when essential and pay off larger amounts such as restaurant bills and pricier items in shops by credit card.

I want to change some pounds/dollars.	**Desidero cambiare delle sterline/dei dollari.**
Do you accept travellers' cheques?	**Accetta travellers cheques?**
Can I pay with a credit card?	**Posso pagare con la carta di credito?**

O

OPENING HOURS

Banks generally open Mon–Fri 8.30am–1.30pm and 2.30–4pm, but the hours vary; a few open continuously from 8am–4pm.

Museums and art galleries vary, some opening all day, others closing for a couple of hours in the afternoon. Closing day is normally Monday.

Churches usually close at lunchtime, from noon to 3pm or later, though the Duomo is open all day.

Shops are generally open Mon–Sat from 9am–1pm and 3.30–7.30pm, but many close on Monday mornings. The large stores in the centre are open all day from 9.30 or 10am–7.30 or 8pm, and sometimes on Sundays too. Food stores close on Monday afternoon. Many shops close in August. For post offices, *see opposite*.

P

POLICE

The city police or *Polizia Urbana* regulate traffic and enforce laws, while the *Carabinieri* are the armed military police who handle law and order. The *Polizia Stradale* patrol the highways and other roads. In an emergency the *Carabinieri* can be reached on 112 – or you can ring the general emergency number, 113. In the case of stolen goods contact the Questura (police station) at Via Fatebenefratelli 11, tel: 02 62261, metro MM3 Turati.

Where's the nearest police station?	**Dov'è il posto di polizia più vicino?**

POST OFFICES

The central post office, offering fax, money transfer and banking facilities, is at Via Cordusio 4, open Mon–Fri 8am–7pm, Sat 8.30am–noon. The Stazione Centrale has a post office with the same opening hours. Most other post offices are open Mon–Fri 8am–2pm, Sat 9.30am–1pm.

Stamps *(francobolli)* can also be purchased from tobacconists (marked with a T sign). First-class mail *(posta prioritaria)* guarantees delivery within 24 hours within Italy and three days for EU countries. Letterboxes are marked *Per la Città* for town mail and *Altre Destinazione* for other destinations. For other information visit <www.poste.it>.

Where's the nearest post office?	**Dov'è l'ufficio postale più vicino?**
I'd like a stamp for this letter/postcard.	**Desidero un francobollo per questa lettera/cartolina.**

PUBLIC HOLIDAYS

Banks, offices, museums, galleries and most shops close on the days listed below. When a national holiday falls on a Friday or a Monday, Italians may make a *ponte* (bridge) or long weekend.

1 January	New Year's Day
6 January	Epiphany
March/April	Easter Monday
25 April	Liberation Day
1 May	Labour Day
15 August	*Ferragosto*, Feast of the Assumption
1 November	All Saints' Day
7 December	Feast of Sant'Ambrogio
8 December	Immaculate Conception
25 December	Christmas Day
26 December	Santo Stefano, St Stephen's Day

PUBLIC TRANSPORT

Milan has an efficient public transport network covering the whole city. The metro is the fastest and most practical means of getting around, allowing you to access most quarters of the city. The public transport system is run by ATM (Azienda Trasporti Milanesi, tel: 800 808181 toll-free in Italy, daily 7.30am–7.30pm, <www.atm-mi.it>).

Metro, Buses and Trams. The Metropolitana Milanese (MM) has three underground lines and a new fast underground railway link known as the Passante Ferroviario. The lines are distinguished by different colours: M1 is red, M2 green, M3 yellow and the link line M4 is blue. A fifth line is under construction, due for completion in 2008. Metro stations are marked by a large red 'M'. Trains run from 6am until 12.30am; there is a train roughly every two minutes at rush hour, every four to five minutes during the rest of the day. Free maps of the public transport system are available from

Milan airports, railway stations, the tourist information office in Piazza del Duomo (see TOURIST INFORMATION) or the ATM office in the Duomo metro station.

Tickets are available from machines at stations, tobacconists and newsagents, and are also valid for tram and bus routes. A single ticket costs €1 and is valid for 75 minutes for one metro journey plus unlimited tram and bus routes. Savings can be made by buying a book of 10 tickets. Tourist tickets, valid for 24 or 48 hours (€3 and €5.50 respectively) can be used on the ATM bus, tram and metro network. Tickets must be validated every time you board a train or bus. Failure to do so may incur a fine.

Trains. Milan's main railway station is the Stazione Centrale (Central Station), a major rail junction with services to cities throughout Italy and the rest of Europe. The station is undergoing a three-year renovation project, due to finish in 2009. Train information can easily be accessed on the Ferrovia dello Stato (State Railway) website at <www.trenitalia.com> (tel: 892021) or, if you're prepared for long queues, from the information office within the station.

Italian trains are cheap compared to those of the UK and the US. The price of a journey depends on the type of train. The fast Eurocity and Intercity trains normally levy a supplement of at least 30 percent, and require seat reservations. The less comfortable Diretto (D), InterRegionale (IR) and Regionale (REG) are slower and cheaper trains, used on more peripheral routes and stopping at local stations. For any of the services it is a good idea to buy your ticket early (at least the day before), as the ticket office invariably has long queues, and buying on board incurs a very hefty supplement. Alternatively, you can use one of the automatic ticket-issuing machines which have clear instructions in English. Return tickets offer no saving on two singles. Before boarding the train, tickets must be franked at the yellow machines at the near end of the platform. Failure to do so may result in a fine.

There are regular fast train services from Milan to towns on the lakes, such as Stresa and Como, and to the historical towns of Lombardy.

When's the next bus/train to…?	**Quando parte il prossimo autobus/treno per…?**
single (one-way)	**andata**
return	**andata e ritorno**
first/second class	**prima/seconda classe**
What's the fare to…?	**Qual è la tariffa per…?**

Taxis. Taxis are white and can be found at ranks around the city. For a Radio Taxi tel: 02 4040, 02 8585 or 02 8383, or call 848 814781 from a land line to be connected to the taxi rank closest to the place you are calling from. There are extra charges on Sundays and holidays, at night and for luggage. Make sure the taxi has a meter and uses it, and beware of touts without meters near airports and train stations.

R

RELIGION

Like the rest of Italy, Milan is primarily Roman Catholic. There are congregations of all the main religions (for details visit <www.hello milano.com> under the 'Worship' section in Useful Information). Access is not allowed to the Duomo if you are dressed in sleeveless shirts, short shorts or other skimpy attire.

S

SMOKING

In January 2005, Italy became the third country in Europe (after Ireland and Norway) to ban smoking in indoor public places. This includes bars and restaurants, unless they have allocated a separate area for smokers.

T

TELEPHONES

Despite the abundance of mobile phones, Telecom Italia public telephones are still widespread. Most of these take prepaid phone cards (*scheda* or *carta telefónica*), available in denominations of €2.50, €5, €10 and €20 from Telecom offices, tobacconists, newsstands and automatic vending machines. Remember to tear off the corner of the card before use. Some Telecom public phones also accept payment by credit card.

Prepaid international telephone cards (from €5), available at post offices, travel agents and other outlets, are better value if you are phoning abroad. With these you call a freephone number, dial the PIN code on your card and then the number (clear instructions are given in English). Calls can also be made with a charge card bought from your telephone company prior to travel. This is useful for telephoning from hotels which levy hefty surcharges on long-distance calls.

When phoning abroad, dial the international code, followed by the city or area code and then the number. The off-peak rate for international calls in Italy is Mon–Sat 10pm–8am, Sun 1pm–Mon 8am. For an English-speaking operator and international reverse-charge calls dial 170, and for international directory enquiries dial 176. Numbers beginning 800 are free. Italian area codes have all been incorporated into the numbers, so even if you are calling from the same town you are telephoning, the code must be included. Note that Italian telephone numbers do not have a standard number of digits – it can be anything from four to ten.

Mobile Phones. In order to function within Italy, some mobile phones need to be activated with a roaming facility or be 'unblocked' for use abroad. Check with your mobile company before leaving home. Charges for using a UK-based mobile to make and receive calls and texts abroad are notoriously high, so it is worth checking with your phone company how much you will be paying and which local network gives the best value. You can then set it to the cheapest network on arrival. You can also bar incoming calls or, on some mobiles, limit them to specified numbers.

If you are in Italy for some time it's worth purchasing an Italian SIM 'pay as you go' *(scheda pre-pagata)* with a new mobile number for the length of your stay. To do so you will need your passport or ID card. The SIM card can be bought from any mobile shop in Italy; if you want to keep your mobile number, sign up with <www.uk2abroad.com> who will divert calls to your Italian SIM card.

Country Codes. Australia +61; Ireland +353; Italy +39; New Zealand +64; UK +44; US and Canada +1.

TIME DIFFERENCES

Italy is one hour ahead of Greenwich Mean Time (GMT). From the last Sunday in March to the last Sunday in October, clocks are put ahead one hour.

The box below shows times across the globe when it is midday in Milan.

New York	London	**Milan**	Jo'burg	Sydney
6am	11am	**noon**	1pm	8pm

TIPPING

In restaurants a *coperto* or cover charge ranging from €1.50–€4 is usually charged for service and bread. Tipping is not taken for granted in Italy, though a bit extra will always be appreciated. For quick service in bars, leave a coin or two with your till receipt when ordering. In restaurants 10 percent is ample. Taxi drivers do not expect a tip, but will appreciate it if you round up the fare to the next euro. At hotels and airports tip porters €1 for each bag.

Thank you, this is for you.	**Grazie, questo è per lei.**
Keep the change.	**Tenga il resto.**

TOILETS

Main train and bus stations have public toilets, usually with attendants who charge a small fee. Otherwise, it is generally a case of using the facilities of a café or bar. To avoid embarrassment, remember that *Signori* is Men, *Signore* is Women.

Where are the toilets, please?	**Dove sono i gabinetti, per favore?**

TOURIST INFORMATION

The Italian National Tourist Office (ENIT, Ente Nazionale Italiano per il Turismo, <www.enit.it>) publishes brochures with tourist information on Milan.

Italian Tourist Offices Abroad
Australia: 44 Market Street, NSW 2000, Sydney, tel: 02 9262 1666, email: <italia@italiantourism.com.au>.
Canada: Suite 907, South Tower, 175 Bloor Street East, Toronto, Ontario M4W3R8, tel: 416-925 4882, <www.italiantourism.com>.
UK: 1 Princes Street, London W1B 2AY, tel: 020 7408 1254, <www.enit.it>.
US: New York: 630 Fifth Avenue, Suite 1565, New York, NY 10111, tel: 212-245 4822 (the common website is <www.italian tourism.com>).

Chicago: 500 North Michigan Avenue, Suite 2240, Chicago, IL 60611, tel: 312-644 0996.
Los Angeles: 12400 Wilshire Boulevard, Suite 550, Los Angeles, CA 90025, tel: 310-820 1898.

Milan Tourist Offices
The central tourist office in Milan, IAT (Informazioni e Assistenza Turistica) is now at Piazza del Duomo 19/A (tel: 02 72524301, email: <iat.info@provincia.milano.it>, <www.milanoinfotourist.it>), close to the Carlo Erba pharmacy. It has recently moved from the building (the Arengario) on the corner of Piazza del Duomo and Via Marconi, which is planned to become part of a major modern art gallery complex *(see page 32)*.

The office supplies a variety of free maps and booklets, such as *Milano Mese* with useful listings and *Hello Milano*, an Italian/English guide in newspaper form packed with information. It's available from some hotels as well as tourist offices (also online at <www.hellomilano.it>). Staff will provide hotel information, but tourists have to make the actual reservation.

The Stazione Centrale (Central Station) has an affiliated IAT tourist office (tel: 02 77404318/4319, open Monday to Saturday 8am–7pm, Sunday 9am–12.30pm and 1.30–6pm.) Milan's airports at Linate, Malpensa and Orio as Serio all have tourist information offices.

W

WEBSITES AND INTERNET

Milan's official site is <www.milanoinfotourist.it>. Other official sites include <www.turismo.comune.milano.it>, which has some stunning virtual tours of all the main sights as well as practical information on all aspects of the city, and <www.comune.milano.it>, mainly aimed at residents but with a useful section in English (click on 'Welcome to Milano') and <www.milano-italy.it>. The most informative English-language website for visitors, covering all aspects of the city, is <www.hellomilano.com>; another excellent English-language site is <www.ciaomilano.com>.

You can use the internet facilities in most hotels – though often there is a charge for doing so – and many of the more upmarket hotels offer wi-fi. Other internet points can be found in cyber cafés, which are open all day and evening, or in offices with internet access for the public, which close during the lunch break. The tourist office *(see above)* can supply a list of internet points in the city, or you can visit <www.comune.milano.it> (Italian only) which lists free and paying internet points. A passport or ID is often required for internet use.

There are internet points at the airports, Stazione Centrale, the Galleria Vittorio Emanuele II and the Mondadori Multicenter, Via Marghera 28 (tel: 02 480 47501), a multimedia centre with long opening hours and 20 internet points.

WEIGHTS AND MEASURES

Italy uses the metric system.

Y

YOUTH HOSTELS

Milan has several official youth hostels. An HI (Hostelling International) card is required, but temporary on-the-spot membership is available. For information and reservations log on to <www.ostellionline.org>.

The city's main hostel is Ostello Piero Rotta, Viale Salmoiraghi 1 (tel: 02 39267095) in the northwest of the city. More central and appealing is La Cordata, Via Burigozzo 11, off Corso Italia (tel: 02 58314675, <www.lacordata.it>), with dormitories, cheap double rooms, use of kitchen, TV room and free use of internet.

Recommended Hotels

Milan's hotels are among the most expensive in Italy. A large number cater for business travellers on expense accounts, and the emphasis is on facilities such as high-speed internet access and fitness centres. Small, charming hotels and budget accommodation are hard to find. The cheapest hotels are near the station, northeast of the centre. It is not the most salubrious area, but is well served by city transport.

You can cut costs dramatically if you are willing to stay in one of the modern hotels several miles outside the city centre. For example, a four-star hotel close to Malpensa airport with shuttle service to the centre could be half the price of its central equivalent. Special weekend rates can be found at hotels which cater for business travellers during the week, and prices drop considerably during August when the Milanese head for the coast. Many of the best rates and special offers are only available online. During the top fashion and design shows (mid-January, mid-February, April, end of June and end of September) prices rocket, and you will need to book months in advance. The same problem can occur in August, when many of the hotels close down.

The symbols below are a rough indication of the cost of a twin room with bathroom, including breakfast, tax and service, in high season.

€€€€	over €300
€€€	€180–300
€€	€130–180
€	below €130

HISTORIC CENTRE

Gran Duca di York €€€ *Via Moneta 1a, tel: 02 874863, fax: 02 8690344, <www.ducadiyork.com>*. One of Milan's most appealing three-star hotels, set in a 200-year-old historic palace. Completely renovated in 2004, the hotel has attractive yellow-and-ochre guest rooms with designer furnishings, satellite TV and minibars.

Park Hyatt €€€€ *Via Tommaso Grossi 1, tel: 02 88211234, fax: 02 88211235, <www.milan.park.hyatt.com>*. Five-star luxury is combined with elegant contemporary décor. A stone's throw away from Piazza del Duomo, with the Park Bar's windows opening out on to the Galleria Vittorio Emanuele II, the hotel couldn't be more central. The dramatic foyer has a soaring glass dome supported by eight columns – La Cupola here offers all-day dining and has become a popular rendezvous for Milanese. The ultimate in luxury are the rooftop suites with large terraces offering stunning city views.

Spadari al Duomo €€€ *Via Spadari 11, tel:02 72002371, fax: 02 861184, <www.spadarihotel.com>*. This was one of Milan's first designer hotels. Close to Piazza del Duomo, it is very stylish, with a pretty, pale-blue colour scheme, light walnut furnishings, innovative works of art and a welcoming atmosphere.

Star €€ *Via dei Bossi 5, tel: 02 801501, fax: 02 861787, <www.hotelstar.it>*. A small, family-run hotel which has a great location close to La Scala, the Duomo and the Castello. There are 30 clean, comfortable rooms with whirlpool baths or sauna showers, satellite TVs and computer connections. Breakfasts are generous for the category of hotel, and the service is particularly attentive and helpful.

Straf €€€–€€€€ *Via San Raffaele 3, tel: 02 805081, fax: 02 8909 5294, <www.straf.it>*. Very much a designer hotel, with exposed concrete, burnished brass, high-tech functionality and a cool cocktail bar. There is a large range of guest rooms, including 'relax rooms' with massaging armchair. Standard rooms are far from spacious, but generally speaking it is well priced for the location and category.

Town House Galleria €€€€ *Galleria Vittorio Emanuele II, tel: 02 89058297, fax: 02 713167, <www.townhouse.it>*. Luxury small hotel in the heart of the city, with 25 rooms and suites above Prada in the Galleria arcade. The historic building has been completely renovated, and opened as part of the Town House group in 2006. The service is discreet, and no expense has been spared in the comfort of the rooms.

CASTELLO SFORZESCO AND NORTHWEST

Ariosto €€€ *Via Ariosto 22, tel: 02 4817844, fax: 02 4980516, <www.brerahotels.com>*. Art Nouveau *palazzo* with a quiet inner courtyard and around 50 well-equipped rooms. The rooms overlooking the court are the most desirable – and some have their own sauna and whirlpool. Facilities include the Bistro restaurant, free bikes for guests' use and free internet access in the lobby.

London €–€€ *Via Rovello 3, tel: 02 72020166, fax: 02 8057037, <www.hotel-london-milan.com>*. Pleasantly old-fashioned, family-run hotel, ideally placed on a quiet street between the Castello and the Duomo. Bedrooms are small and nothing special, but there is a convivial lounge, and the staff are extremely helpful and friendly.

BRERA

Antica Locanda Solferino €€–€€€ *Via Castelfidardo 2, tel: 02 6570129, fax: 02 6571361, <www.anticalocandasolferino.it>*. Intimate and friendly little hotel in the heart of the Brera, with an almost rustic feel. The 11 rooms are full of character and a good size, all individually furnished with Art Nouveau antiques, floral fabrics, original prints – along with flat-screen TVs and wi-fi.

NORTHEAST OF CENTRE

Hotel Aspromonte € *Piazza Aspromonte 12/14, tel: 02 2361119, fax: 02 2367621, <www.hotelaspromonte.it>*. This hotel, in an Art Nouveau building overlooking Piazza Aspromonte, offers great value for money. The 19 rooms are furnished in a sober, modern style, and are equipped with internet facilities and satellite TVs. The proprietors are young, and the staff friendly and easygoing. In summer breakfast is served in the interior garden. The location is slightly off the beaten track, but there is a good metro service from nearby Piazzale Loreto.

Baviera €€–€€€ *Via P. Castaldi 7, tel: 02 6590551, fax: 02 29003281, <www.mokinba.it>*. Traditional hotel with helpful, friendly staff, plus rooms that are well equipped and good value.

On a pleasant street just north of the public gardens, it's convenient for the station and has a good choice of restaurants, pizzerias and bars in the surrounding streets.

Bulgari €€€€ *Via Privata Fratelli Gabbia 7b, tel: 02 8058051, fax: 02 805805222, <www.bulgarihotels.com>*. Bulgari of jewellery fame opened this seductive hotel in 2004, and it is now generally regarded as the top hotel in Milan. Luxury and glamour here are combined with bold, contemporary design. Overlooking the Botanical Gardens, and with its own garden and stunning spa and lap pool, it's a great place to relax after a day's retail therapy. Guest rooms throughout are super-stylish, decorated in tones of brown and beige with black furniture. The garden-view, minimalist restaurant attracts an ultra-elegant crowd – particularly during fashion shows, when you need to book a year in advance. Services include a professional personal shopper and a luggage-packing and unpacking service.

Casa Mia € *Viale Vittorio Veneto 30, tel: 02 6575249, fax: 02 6552228, <www.casamiahotel.it>*. Friendly little two-star hotel near the Piazza Repubblica and the Giardini Pubblici (Public Gardens), 15 minutes' walk from the Duomo. There are 15 simply furnished, spotless rooms, all with en suite bathrooms, satellite TV and air conditioning. The street is a busy one, but most rooms overlook a quiet internal courtyard.

Four Seasons €€€€ *Via Gesù 6/8, tel: 02 77088, fax: 02 77085000, <www.fourseasons.com/milan>*. Converted from a 15th-century convent, this exclusive hotel has rooms around a cloistered courtyard and a beautiful lounge retaining the Gothic arches and original frescos. The comforts, service and discreet location on a quiet street amid Italy's most famous fashion salons bring many celebrities. Bedrooms are spacious and luxurious, each one individually furnished.

Grand Hotel et de Milan €€€€ *Via Alessandro Manzoni 29, tel: 02 723141, fax: 02 86460861, <www.grandhoteletdemilan.it>*. A prestigious location a stone's throw from La Scala, sumptuous rooms and impeccable service combine to make this one of the most desirable five-star hotels in the city. Founded in 1863, the hotel has a roll call of illustrious guests including Giuseppe Verdi *(see page 54)*, Ernest Hemingway and Maria Callas.

Nettuno €–€€ *Via Tadino 27, tel: 02 29404481, fax: 02 29523819, <www.nettunomilano.it>.* A friendly base near the central train station. The functional rooms now all have air conditioning and minibars.

Principe di Savoia €€€€ *Piazza della Repubblica 17, tel: 02 62301, fax: 02 6595838, <www.principedisavoia.com>.* The antidote to Milan's many minimalist hotels, the de luxe Principe di Savoia is a grandiose edifice with chandeliers and antiques. Guest rooms in 19th-century style offer every comfort, and the service is impeccable. Of the 401 rooms, 132 are suites. The top-floor spa and fitness centre has a small heated pool, high-tech gym and beauty treatment.

San Francisco € *Viale Lombardia 55, tel: 02 2360302, fax: 02 26680377, <www.hotel-sanfrancisco.it>.* A two-star hotel a few minutes' walk east of the station, and worth the slightly out-of-the-way location for the reasonable prices. Simple, well-cared-for rooms are all equipped with bathroom, air conditioning and TV, there is a bar/breakfast room and – rare for Milan – a leafy garden at the back.

Starhotels Anderson €€–€€€€ *Piazza Luigi di Savoia, tel: 02 6690141, fax: 02 6690331, <www.starhotels.it>.* Literally steps from the railway station, the Anderson makes a convenient and comfortable stopover. Recently refurbished from top to toe, the hotel offers all the latest technology, a fitness centre, which is open 24 hours a day, as well as chic modern rooms with good bathrooms and their own mini flat-screen TVs. The service is courteous and friendly and the food is good.

Town House 31 €€€–€€€€ *Via Carlo Goldoni 31, tel: 02 70156, fax: 02 713167, <www.townhouse.it>.* In a residential quarter out of the historic centre, this is a chic home-from-home for the fashionistas, offering a combination of comfort, cutting-edge design and convivial atmosphere. The style is multicultural: there are Chinese temple arches into the courtyard, oriental darkwood furniture and artefacts in guest rooms, offsetting the cream-and-white décor and African touches. The foyer functions as the breakfast room, with a long communal table, and from 6–9pm as a popular *aperitivo* bar and a tropical garden winebar. Needless to say, this is a hot favourite in fashion weeks.

NORTHWEST/FIERA

Bed and Bread € *Via Vetta d'Italia 14, tel: 02 468267, <www.bedandbread.it>* This B&B south of the trade centre has three double rooms and a communal room with TV, internet and library. Breakfasts are generous and comprise home-made breads, jam and cakes. The Duomo is 2km (1 mile) away and can be reached by bus or tram.

Town House 12 €€€–€€€€ *Piazza Gerusalemme 12, tel: 02 89078511, fax: 02 89078517, <www.townhouse.it>.* Sister hotel of Townhouse 31 and the one in the Galleria *(see above)*, this is close to the trade centre and equally sophisticated and fashionable. There are just 18 rooms in soothing colours, and the comfy lounges have wireless connection. Sociable public areas include the communal breakfast room, the terrace and the Absolut Icebar Milan, created entirely from ice *(see page 92)*.

WEST OF CENTRE

Antica Locanda dei Mercanti €€€ *Via San Tomaso 6, tel: 02 8054080, fax: 02 8054090, <www.locanda.it>.* A gem of a hotel inconspicuously set on a small central street equidistant from the cathedral, castle and designer shops of the Quadrilatero d'Oro. There are 14 gorgeous guest rooms, each one individually furnished with lovely classic fabrics. Optional breakfasts are taken in your room – or in the case of four of the rooms on your private terrace. Unusually the rooms are TV-less – fresh flowers, books and magazines take their place – but wi-fi and broadband access are provided.

Antica Locanda Leonardo €€–€€€ *Corso Magenta 78, tel: 02 48014197, fax: 02 48019012, <www.leoloc.com>.* This is a prime location on the smart Corso Magenta, very close to Leonardo's *The Last Supper*. The hotel is run by a delightful Japanese and Italian couple. Reception is a pretty salon overlooking the courtyard. Bedrooms are a decent size for Milan and simply furnished, mainly with traditional fabrics, 1930s furniture and cherrywood floors.

King €€€ *Corso Magenta 19, tel: 02 874432, fax: 02 89010798, <www.hotelkingmilano.com>.* Civilised and welcoming three-star on the elegant Corso Magenta to the west of the city centre. Rooms have traditional furnishings and floral fabrics. The energetic (and brave) will appreciate the free use of the hotel's bikes.

Palazzo delle Stelline €€€ *Corso Magenta 61, tel: 02 4818431, fax: 02 4851909, <www.hotelpalazzostelline.it>.* A 15th-century monastery and former orphanage, this is now a congress centre/hotel with rooms set around a large cloister. The location is excellent, on the upmarket Corso Magenta, the modern guest rooms are well equipped and there is a choice of food from the café/bar with attractive terrace, the self-service Le Stelline and the gourmet Terrazza di Leonardo restaurant. Rooms are good value given the location, but reception staff could be more welcoming.

SOUTH OF CENTRE

Ariston €–€€ *Largo Carrobbio 2, tel: 02 72000556, fax: 02 72000914, <www.brerahotels.com>.* 'The first ecological hotel', the Ariston provides air-purified rooms, drinks made with purified water, organic breakfast products and free bikes for guests to use to explore the city. The rather dreary looking nine-storey block is set back off a busy street, about a 10-minute walk, or five-minute bike ride, from the Duomo.

Corte del Naviglio €€–€€€ *Via Lodovico il Moro 117, tel: 02 8925777, fax: 02 89155516, <www.cabianca.info>.* A reasonably priced four-star hotel, outside the historic centre, but well served by public transport. Surrounded by a leafy garden, the building was the summer residence of the Marquess of Barona in the 17th century. Pretty guest rooms have tiled floors and are decorated in different shades of yellow and blue; the Cà Bianca on the premises offers evening entertainment.

Recommended Restaurants

Unsurprisingly, Milan has a huge choice of places to eat, from humble trattorias to temples of gastronomy. In addition to Italian fare, there are countless ethnic restaurants, particularly Japanese, Asian, African, Arab and South American. Prices in Milan are higher than the rest of Italy (Venice excepted); for the best value, head for the Ticinese and Navigli quarters in the south of the city. It is advisable to make a reservation at busy times of the year, especially during major trade fairs. Normal opening times for lunch *(pranzo)* are from 12.30pm to 2.30 or 3pm, the evening meal *(cena)* from 7 or 7.30pm to 10pm or 11pm, with some pizzerias and ethnic restaurants staying open until midnight. Most restaurants close for August. Lunch menus, generally featuring lighter fare, are frequently cheaper than those offered at dinner. Restaurants, including many pizzerias, usually add a €1–4 charge for bread and cover *(pane e coperto)*, plus sometimes a 10–15 percent service charge. If service is not included, it is normal to leave a tip. Italians tend to leave no more than a couple of euros unless the service has been spectacular.

The prices indicated are for a three-course evening meal per person, including cover charge and service but excluding wine.

€€€€	over 65 euros
€€€	45–65 euros
€€	25–45 euros
€	below 25 euros

HISTORIC CENTRE

Antico Ristorante Boeucc €€€ *Piazza Belgioioso 2, tel: 02 76020224, <www.boeucc.it>*. The oldest restaurant in Milan, Boeucc started life as a simple *osteria* serving wine and pasta, then transferred to the grandiose Palazzo Belgioioso in 1939. It is close to La Scala opera house, and among its many famous guests were

Verdi, Donizetti and Toscanini. Nowadays, popular with businessmen as well as artists, it is renowned for impeccable service and classic Milanese cuisine. Try the delicious *antipastino caldo del pescatore*, a hot fish hors d'oeuvre based on a recipe given to the restaurant by Toscanini, the saffron-flavoured *risotto alla milanese* (Milan risotto), or the *costolettine di capretto con carciofi*, kid cutlets with artichokes. Closed Saturday and Sunday lunch.

Cracco Peck €€€€ *Via Victor Hugo 4, tel: 02 876774.* Arguably the best restaurant in Milan, opened in 2000 by chef Carlo Cracco from Vicenza and awarded two Michelin stars for outstanding innovative cuisine. The *menu degustazione* gives you the opportunity to try several of the specialities. The desserts are legendary, and the wine list outstanding. If you can't afford the prices (and they're very steep), try their more informal restaurant, Italian Bar *(see below)*, or, cheaper still, a take-away from the Peck deli *(see page 87)*. Closed Saturday lunch and Sunday.

Italian Bar €€ *Via Cesare Cantù 3, tel: 02 8693017.* Fashionable modern bar/bistro under the same management as Cracco Peck and open continuously from 11.30am–8.30pm for light meals, coffee and pastries or cocktails. At lunchtime it's especially popular with employees from the nearby Stock Exchange. There are serious wines from the Peck cellars, and a good choice of cheeses and cold cuts to go with them. Closed Sunday.

Luini € *Via Santa Radegonda 16, tel: 02 86461917, <www.luini.it>.* Very close to the Duomo, this is a small, crowded bakery specialising in *panzerotto*, the freshly made Puglian pastry folded over fillings of tomato and mozzarella, ricotta, ham and spinach or other ingredients. No credit cards. Open Tues–Sat 10am–8pm, Mon 10am–3pm, closed Sunday.

Al Mercante €€€ *Piazza Mercanti 17, tel: 02 8052198.* Lovely spot on the only medieval square in Milan. This is a remodelled Gothic building with tables on the square under large, white canopies. It is popular with local businessmen as well as tourists, and has delicious home-made pasta and fresh fish. Closed Sunday.

La Milanese €€–€€€ *Via Santa Marta 11, tel: 02 86451991.* Genuine Milanese fare is served in this traditional trattoria, and has been since 1919 when the Villa family took it over. You can always find *osso buco* (braised veal shanks) *risotto alla milanese, cotoletta alla milanese* (breaded and fried veal), plus other seasonal specialities. Excellent choice of Lombard wines. Closed Tuesday.

Le Terrazze €€ *La Rinascente, Via Santa Radegonda 3, tel: 02 877159.* On the seventh floor of Milan's most prestigious department store, it's the views of the Duomo roof you come for rather than the food. Try to sit outside to get close to the pinnacles. As well as lunch and supper, coffee, cakes, aperitifs and nibbles are served at any time of day. Closed Sunday lunch and Monday.

CASTELLO SFORZESCO AND NORTHWEST

ATMosfera €€ *tel: freephone 800 808181 (within Italy), <www.atm-mi.it>.* For an evening with a difference, dine in a plushly furnished, old-fashioned tram which takes you around the city and down to the Navigli quarter. There are two set menus, one meat-based and one fish-based, each costing €50 including wine. Reservations, online or by telephone, should be made by 7.30pm the day before you want to dine. The departure point is Piazza Castello. No tours on Monday.

Coffee Design € *La Triennale di Milano, Viale Alemagna 6, tel: 02 875441, <www.coffeedesign.it>.* Trendy café at the Triennale overlooking Parco Sempione, furnished with 50 different designer chairs and changing pieces of international industrial design. Serves snacks and light lunches, cocktails at Happy Hour and Sunday brunch. Closed Monday.

Quattro Mori €€€ *Largo Maria Callas, tel: 02 878483.* Close to Castello Sforzesco, this is an inviting restaurant where you can eat on a shady terrace or inside in the mirrored salon. *Antipasti*, fish and desserts are spread out for you to choose. The menu caters for all tastes, with plenty of pasta, fish and meat, and a good range of salads. Closed Saturday lunch.

BRERA

Da Claudio € *Via Ponte Vetero 16, tel: 02 8056857.* Wonderful value and invariably crowded fish and sushi bar. Oysters, scallops, marinated salmon and raw mixed fish are typically washed down with chilled *Spumante* (or Champagne). Standing room only. Closed Sunday and Monday.

Latteria San Marco €–€€ *Via San Marco 24, tel: 02 6597653.* This is one of the last *latterie*, or dairy shops. Small and homely, it serves simple Lombard fare and is frequented by journalists from the nearby *Corriere della Sera* newspaper. No credit cards or bookings. Closed Saturday and Sunday.

Nabucco €€€ *Via Fiori Chiari 10, tel: 02 860663.* Elegant cuisine in the atmospheric heart of the Brera. Dine by candlelight, and alfresco on summer evenings. Try Nabucco's *antipasti*, the sautéed *zucchini* (courgette) flowers filled with risotto and pesto, spaghetti with rock lobster, or the fresh fish which arrives daily. The restaurant is open until 11.30pm and is a popular post-theatre venue.

Torre di Pisa €€ *Via Fiora Chiari 21, tel: 02 874877.* Tuscan trattoria with rustic setting on a lively street of the Brera, serving delicious steaks. Closed Sunday.

NORTHEAST OF CENTRE

Alistair's Vini e Cucina €€ *Via Panfilo Castaldi 38, tel: 02 29519840.* Alistair Parker came to Milan as a young English teacher, but fell in love with cooking and, now as a successful chef with his own wine bar/restaurant, has proved to the Milanese that British cooking isn't all bad. Along with high-quality Mediterranean fare he offers classy fish and chips in Guinness batter, steak and kidney pie, Sunday roast with Yorkshire pudding – and also weekend brunches. Closed Monday.

Bice €€ *Via Borgospesso 12, tel: 02 76002572, <www.bicemilano. it>.* In the heart of the exclusive shopping quarter, this is a favourite spot for fashionable Milanese. Elegant cuisine featuring Tuscan as well as traditional local dishes. Closed Sunday.

Brek € *Via dell'Annunciata 2, Piazza Cavou, tel: 02 653619, <www.brek.it>*. This is an excellent-value chain where you help yourself to pastas, pizza and risottos, freshly made hot dishes, salads and fresh fruit. Red, white and sparkling wines are available on tap. The self-service style is uncharacteristic of Italy, but the setting is pleasant, and this is the one place you can be assured of a bill without a cover or service charge (and no language problems either!). There is another branch at Via Lepetit 20, near the central station.

Corso Como 10 €€ *Corso Como 10, tel 02 29013581*. Part of an ultra-fashionable shopping emporium, this bar/restaurant in an elegant courtyard serves a great Sunday brunch, as well as sushi and a few other international dishes.

Cova € *Via Montenapoleone 8, tel 02 6000578*. Ideal spot for a coffee and brioche break while you're shopping in the Quadrilatero d'Oro. This elegant *pasticceria*, dating back nearly 200 years, is famous for its *panettone* (the Milanese Christmas cake) and mouth-watering chocolate cake.

Da Giannino-L'Angolo d'Abruzzo €€ *Via Pilo 20, tel: 02 29406526*. The same family have been running this charming, old-fashioned trattoria for 45 years. You can expect a warm welcome and hearty portions of cuisine from the Abruzzo region here. Closed Monday.

Joia €€–€€€ *Via Panfilo Castaldi 18, tel: 02 29522124, <www.joia.it>*. Gastronomic vegetarian fare in a modern, elegant setting just north of the Giardini Pubblici (Public Gardens). The menu may take a while to work out with its capriciously named delicacies such as *Il tonno e la sua ombra* (tuna fish and its shadow), *Il Pianeta Verde va verso il su centro* (Towards the core of the Green Planet) and *L'Uovo Apparente* (The Apparent Egg). Everything is carefully cooked to order (allow plenty of time for a meal here), and menus use the freshest ingredients. Seafood dishes are also served. It's advisable to book at least a week in advance. Closed Sunday and Saturday lunch.

Nobu €€€€ *Via Pisoni 1, tel: 02 62318645*. Within the Armani megastore and part of the chain of Japanese master chef Nobuyuki Matsuhisa. Fashionistas flock here for the fusion cuisine – with Japanese and South American influences. The downstairs Nobu sushi cocktail bar is far cheaper than upstairs. Closed Sunday and lunch on Monday.

Ombre Rosse € *Via Plinio 29, tel: 02 29524734, <www.enoteca ombrerosse.com>*. A wine bar since the 1930s, when lorries came with tankfuls of Chianti, the Ombre Rosse today offers a selection of 400 wines. To accompany them are Tuscan and Parma hams, salted and smoked pork and salami, pâté de foie gras, *pasta e fagioli* (pasta and beans), cassoulet or vegetable couscous. For wine by the glass you can choose from around a dozen recommendations which are listed on the blackboard, and changed weekly. Closed Sunday lunch and Monday.

Il Teatro €€€€ *Four Seasons Hotel, Via Gesù 6–8, tel: 02 77088, <www.fourseasons.com/milan>*. Save this one for a special occasion. Exquisite dishes are served in the restaurant of the five-star Four Seasons Hotel, overlooking a beautiful cloistered courtyard. Regional, seasonal, vegetarian and children's menus are offered as well as à la carte.

WEST OF CENTRE

Da Leo €€ *Via Trivulzio 26, tel: 02 40071445*. A family-run Pugliese trattoria, which serves the freshest of fish cooked in traditional dishes of the region. It has a friendly atmosphere. Closed Monday and dinner on Sunday.

Kota Radja €€–€€€ *Piazzale Baracca 6, tel: 02 468850*. One of the first Chinese restaurants to open in Milan; also one of the best and most expensive. Cantonese cuisine.

Il Luogo di Aimo e Nadia €€€€ *Via Montecuccoli 6, tel: 02 416886, <www.aimoenadia.com>*. Aimo and Nadia's Place is well off the tourist track, a modest restaurant out in the suburbs, but a favourite haunt of serious food-lovers. The Tuscan husband-and-wife team are renowned for their innovative cuisine, using the very freshest of ingredients. With simple, modern décor, the graffiti-like art hanging on the white walls may not be to your taste but the delicious traditional dishes are unlikely to disappoint. Closed Sunday and lunch on Saturday.

Yume €€€ *Via Varesina 215, tel: 02 3089045*. North of the Fiera-Milano City trade centre, this Japanese restaurant was created by a feng shui expert. Come for the Zen experience, and the melt-in-the-mouth sushi and sashimi cooked in front of you.

SOUTH OF CENTRE

Asso di Fiori €–€€ *Alzaia Naviglio Grande 54*. An *osteria* specialising in cheese. Choose from a variety of vegetarian and meat dishes with cheese sauces, a *Degustazione Formaggi* (Cheese Tasting) menu or a platter of cheeses with delicious breads. If that all sounds too much, you can just opt for a simply grilled steak. Closed Sunday and lunch on Saturday.

Guilio Pane e Ojo €€ *Via L. Muratori 10, tel: 02 5456189, <www.giuliopaneojo.com>*. Small and inviting *osteria* specialising in robust Roman cuisine. Good value. Outdoor seating in summer. Closed Sunday.

Joia Leggero €€ *Corso di Porta Ticinese 106, tel: 02 89404134, <www.joia.it>*. Sister restaurant to the Joia restaurant near the Public Gardens *(see page 139)*, but with lower prices and a younger crowd. Minimalist décor and delectable vegetarian and seafood creations. Closed Sunday and lunch on Monday.

Marghera 37 €–€€ *Via Marghera 37, tel: 02 4814368*. Sophisticated lounge bar and restaurant serving breakfast, lunch, cocktails, dinner, post-theatre Mediterranean meals and Sunday brunch. Closed Wednesday.

Al Merluzzo Felice €€–€€€ *Via Lazzaro Papi 6, tel: 02 5454711.* A tiny and inconspicuous but welcoming restaurant off the beaten track (you have to ring the doorbell to enter). Outstanding for its Sicilian specialities, fish, pasta and mouth-watering desserts. Closed Sunday and lunch on Monday.

Pizzeria Tradizionale €€ *Corsa di Porta Ticinese 7, tel: 02 8395133.* Excellent fish and fresh pasta are served here, as well as traditional Neapolitan-style pizzas. Expect baked scallops *au gratin*, pasta with seafood and asparagus, fish soups, grilled swordfish, salted seabass or mixed grilled fish. Desserts are all homemade and use natural ingredients. It is open until midnight and usually packed. Closed Wednesday

Al Pont de Ferr €€ *Ripa di Porta Ticinese 55, tel: 02 89406277.* Hugely popular and very welcoming wood-panelled *osteria*, one of the few in the Navigli (canal) quarter which is open all day every day. Among the starters and *primi* are *affettati misti* (cold sliced salami, parma ham and *pancetta*) served with home-made bread and honey and pear sauce; home-made foie gras, ravioli filled with mozzarella, tomato and basil, risotto with fresh *vongole* and *polpo* (clams and octopus). Meat predominates on the main courses; there are home-made desserts and a tempting selection of cheeses to finish.

Premiata Pizzeria €–€€ *Alzaia Naviglio Grande 2, tel: 02 89400648.* Exceptionally good pizzeria at the Darsena end of the canal, with garden and terrace. Choose from 42 different types of pizza, which come bubbling from a wood-fired oven. Other options are *focaccia*, cured meats, cheeses, pastas, steaks or salads.

Sadler €€€€ *Via Ettore Troilo 14, angolo Via Conchetta (near the Navigli), tel: 02 58104451, <www.sadler.it>.* A Milanese temple of gastronomy, awarded two Michelin stars for Claudio Sadler's creative and beautifully presented cuisine. The menu is based on the freshest of seasonal fare and changes on a regular basis. The *Menu Desgustazione* will give you the opportunity to taste a whole range of specialities. Dinner only and closed on Sunday.

INDEX

Abbazia di Chiaravalle 76
accommodation 107, 109, 127, 128–34
airports 108
Arco della Pace 45
Arena Civica 45

Bars 91–2
Basilica di San Lorenzo Maggiore 72
Basilica di Sant'Ambrogio 65, 95
Basilica di Sant'Eustorgio 70–1, 95
Brera, The 48–51, 84, 88, 91

Ca'Grande (University of Milan) 74
Cappella di San Vittore in Ciel d'Oro 65
Cappella Portinari 70–1
Cappella Sant' Aquilino 73
Casa degli Omenoni 36
Casa di Alessandro Manzoni 36
Casa Fontana-Silvestri 58
Castello Sforzesco 40–4, 91
castle museums 42–4
Cimitero Monumentale 47
Civica Galleria d'Arte Moderna 56
Civiche Raccolte d'Arte Applicata 44
Civico Museo Archeologico 63

Darsena 69
Duomo 25–30

Entertainment 88–92

Festivals 95
Food and drink 87, 96–105

Galleria Vittorio Emanuele II 33, 86
Giardini Pubblici 56, 95
Grand Hotel et de Milan 54, 131

Isola 47

Just Cavalli Café 46, 92

La Scala *(see Teatro alla Scala)*
Last Supper, The 58–61
Leonardo da Vinci 19, 35, 38, 43, 58–61, 62, 63, 67, 77

Madonnina 26, 28
Monza 80–1, 93, 95
Museo Bagatti Valsecchi 53
Museo Civico di Storia Naturale 42, 56–7
Museo degli Strumenti Musicali 44
Museo del Cinema 56
Museo del Duomo 32
Museo del Risorgimento 42, 55
Museo della Reggia 32
Museo di Milano 55

Index

Museo di Storia Contemporanea 55
Museo Diocesano 71
Museo Nazionale della Scienza e della Tecnologia Leonardo da Vinci 62
Museo Poldi Pezzoli 54–5
Museo Teatrale alla Scala 35

Navigli, The 66–70, 84, 88, 91, 95
nightclubs 91–2

Padiglione d'Arte Contemporanea 56
Palazzo Castiglioni 57–8
Palazzo dell'Arte (Triennale) 46
Palazzo della Ragione 36–7
Palazzo di Giustizia 74
Palazzo Marino 35
Palazzo Reale 30–3
Palazzo Rocca-Saporiti 57
Palazzo Serbelloni 58
Parco dell'Anfiteatro 73
Parco Sempione 45–6
Pavia 77–8
    Basilica di San Michele 78
    Certosa di Pavia 78–80
Piazza del Duomo 30
Piazza della Scala 35
Piazza Mercanti 36–7
Pinacoteca Ambrosiana 38–9
Pinacoteca di Brera 48–50
Pirelli Tower 11, 26
Planetario 'Ulrico Hoepli' 57
Porta Ticinese 68
public transport 120

Quadrilatero d'Oro 52–3, 83

Raccolta dei Mobili 43
restaurants 135–42
Rondanini Pietà 43

San Gottardo in Corte 31
San Lorenzo alle Colonne 72–3
San Marco 51
San Maurizio 64, 91
San Nazaro Maggiore 74
San Simpliciano 51
Sant'Ambrogio 14, 15, 65
Santa Maria dei Carmine 51
Santa Maria delle Grazie 58–61
Santa Maria Presso San Satiro 39
shopping 83–8
sport 93–4

Teatro alla Scala 34–5, 54, 89–90, 95
Torre Branca 46, 92
Torre Velasca 75
tourist information 125
Triennale (Palazzo dell'Arte) 46

Università Statale 74

Verdi, Giuseppe 54
Vicolo del Lavandai 70

Youth hostels 127